David Williams

Letters on political liberty, and the principles of the English and Irish projects of reform

addressed to a member of the English House of Commons. Third Edition

David Williams

Letters on political liberty, and the principles of the English and Irish projects of reform

addressed to a member of the English House of Commons. Third Edition

ISBN/EAN: 9783744740616

Printed in Europe, USA, Canada, Australia, Japan

Cover: Foto ©ninafisch / pixelio.de

More available books at **www.hansebooks.com**

LETTERS

ON

POLITICAL LIBERTY,

AND THE PRINCIPLES OF THE

ENGLISH AND IRISH

PROJECTS OF REFORM;

ADDRESSED TO

A MEMBER OF THE

ENGLISH HOUSE OF COMMONS.

THIRD EDITION.

Deerant quoque littora ponto. Ov.

LONDON:

PRINTED FOR J. RIDGWAY, YORK-STREET,
ST. JAMES'S-SQUARE.

M.DCC.LXXXIX.

[Price Two Shillings and Sixpence.]

CONTENTS.

LETTER I.
Reasons for writing these Letters,   Page 1

LETTER II.
Nature of Political Liberty, — 6

LETTER III.
Short History of Political Liberty in England, — — 12

LETTER IV.
View of the Administration of Government, in the Reign of George the Third, as far as the Subject is concerned, — — 17

LETTER V.
View of the Conduct of Parties in Opposition to the Administration of George the Third, at the Time of writing these Letters, — — 25

CONTENTS.

LETTER VI.

The Method of introducing, establishing, or recovering a State of Political Liberty, —— —— 37

LETTER VII.

Plan of an equal Representation of the People of England, —— 57

Letters to the associated Correspondents of a periodical Paper, called, The Friend of the People, 69, &c.

LETTERS

ON

POLITICAL LIBERTY.

LETTER I.

Reasons for writing these Letters.

DEAR SIR,

I THINK no period in the annals of England, has afforded objects so numerous and interesting, as those which now employ its attention.

Whether the evils we endure, and the greater evils we apprehend, are owing to errors and faults of particular Administrations perverting the powers of an excellent Constitution; or the government of England be a confused combination of heterogeneous and discordant principles;

ples: are questions forced on the judgement of all men.

Persons in high offices, senators, and lawyers, claim an exclusive right of judging on these questions; because they have had experience, and possess knowledge of facts: but the claim is the effect of imposture, or of inacquaintance with the subject. Government, as an art, may be best understood by those who discharge its offices, or employ their faculties in distinguishing and enforcing its injunctions: but the principles of government constitute a profound and arduous *science*; and to combine or harmonize them, is the employment of the sublimest understandings, using experience or facts as the materials of deliberate contemplation.

Without incurring the imputation of vanity, by appearing to arrange myself in this order of men, I may attempt to draw their attention to the subject of the following Letters; by exhibiting it in a new light, or under a denomination becoming its importance.

I do not recollect a writer who has treated Politics as a science, and deduced his demonstrations from clear or indisputable data. Government

ment has been referred to the appointment of Deities; to the regulations of Patriarchs; to the physical influence of climates; to the ebullition of accidental circumstances producing the spirit of nations; to divine rights in favored families; to superiority of talents; to the prevalence of force; and to a compact, tacit or express, of the governors and the governed.

If Government be referrable to either of these causes; it has no sure or indisputable principles, in common with other sciences: but if it be the institution of men, to obtain security and happiness, it is to be considered as any other contrivance, the parts of which are constructed on principles. The savages of America imagined ships to be the vehicles of immortal spirits; and a shipwreck on their coasts may have occasioned disputes as perplexing, or argumentations as subtle, as those in Europe by the decomposition of ancient governments.

It is time to discard the reveries of savages, and to apply principles of science to all scientific objects. As in the construction of machines, it is necessary to arrange and estimate the forces of combinations, to produce general effects; so in Government, first principles must be discovered, or all disquisitions will be vague: the pretensions of all impostors in the arts of administration will be equally plausible; and remedies for its disorders be offered at random, or applied with hazard.

Politics, assuming the rank of science, would not be left to men of business, whose active faculties may be astonishing; as their powers of reflection must be inconsiderable. Philosophers, in the habit of combining first principles, would leave the barren labyrinths of metaphysics, or the futile legerdemain of minute experiments: and seeing the existence of other sciences depending on the construction of Governments, they would ascertain their principles; harmonize combinations; and point out remedies of errors incident to all the productions of human abilities. At this time, the greatest men in every state, are passengers in vessels conducted by ignorant mariners; and apply themselves to any thing but the science on which their safety depends: when these vessels are lost, philosophers are sunk in the abyss, in common with the most contemptible reptiles. The first concern of every man should be, the nature and construction of the machine in which he is embarked on the voyage of life; other interests or pursuits obtaining only secondary attentions.

This

This is my reason for directing my thoughts to political subjects: and I address them to you, because in conversations I have lately had with you, it appeared you did not view the steps and prospects of Associated Counties, Parliamentary Inquiries, and City Remonstrances, with a mind unembarrassed, or with hopes of success. Your desire to know what I could offer on the occasion, is an inducement to commit to paper, thoughts which otherwise might have continued floating in my mind. I am assured of your candid attention; and that the utmost use in your power will be made of any sentiments I may suggest. Had my object been to instruct the leaders of parties, I should have found prepossessions or interests in my way; and have lost that species of time, which is to me the most precious of all possessions.

If, on perusing the Letters, you should not be informed or benefitted; you will not be displeased with them as testimonies of the respect and esteem with which I am,

SIR,

Your sincere, and
most humble servant.

March 4, 1782.

LETTER II.

Nature of Political Liberty.

De minoribus principes consultant; de majoribus, omnes.
Their chiefs deliberated on lesser matters; on greater, the whole nation.   T<small>AC</small>. de Mor. Germ.

ALL disputes might be prevented by clear or honest definitions; yet most men dislike the effort of attending to them. I shall avoid every definition, not absolutely necessary to the purpose of these Letters.

If writers on Government had made and preserved the distinction of Civil and Political Liberty, my trouble would have been unnecessary; and I should have entered on other parts of my subject.*

Civil Liberty is the result of laws or regulations, which define the boundaries of men's actions as citizens of the same community, and

---

* Montesquieu made a distinction of civil and political liberty; but not similar to that of the author: and he has in no case adhered to it.

leave

leave them free within those boundaries. Political Liberty is the result of incidents or institutions combining the grand divisions of the State; the popular, the executive, and the legislative; and consists in their freedom from the incroachments of each other. A community has no political Liberty, when the executive power influences or commands the legislature; or when the people have not regular and practical methods of checking or controuling all the branches of Government into their proper boundaries. A society may enjoy civil Liberty, i. e. all interference of individuals may be regulated by laws; while no method may be ascertained to regulate the several branches of Government; to prevent the encroachments of any or all of them on the power and happiness of the whole people. We shall see, that England furnishes reasons for fixing the public attention on this important distinction. Since the Revolution, and the accession of the Hanover Family, its civil Liberties have been improved, while political Liberty has been nearly annihilated: its constitution, therefore, is among the most aukward and unmanageable fabrics which have been produced by human talents.

That political Liberty is essential to a wise or happy constitution of government, is demonstrable;

ble; as that three lines are neceſſary to form a triangle.

All bodies, natural or political, have a principle of ſelf-preſervation reſulting from their conſtruction; from the union and harmony of their parts: without which they ceaſe to exiſt. The offices of the members are diſtinct; and they cannot be blended, without inconvenience and miſchief. In communities, the legiſlative power deliberates and ordains; the executive puts the laws in force *for the whole body*; which muſt have a principle of ſelf-preſervation, not only on account of other communities, but to provide againſt the erroneous or miſchievous exertions of its own members. Power, without a refiſting or balancing power, is like a muſcle without its antagoniſt; which always diſtorts, and may occaſion fatal diſorders. Legiſlation and magiſtracy, without actual power in the people to preſerve their Liberty, are abſurdities; or they are maſques for the features of deſpotiſm.

A ſtate, properly conſtituted, muſt have a body of men to make laws; a perſon or perſons to repreſent the community to foreign nations, and to execute the laws for the preſervation of civil Liberty; and a power reſerved by the people

ple to repel encroachments, or to confine the members of the community within the limits of their offices.

This truth, though not deemed fusceptible of demonstration, has been admitted by political writers; those excepted, who avow their attachment to despotism. I am not ashamed to decline all contest with the advocates of despotism. If the happiness of the world had nothing to apprehend but their arguments, it would be well. The most dangerous enemies of Liberty are of its own houshold. Every witling, from Solon to the declamatory retainer of an English faction, pretends to distinguish between theory and practice. It has ever been the expedient of knaves and blockheads. If in geometry, all clear and accurate demonstrations are reducible to practice, why not in politics?—These gentlemen cannot tell: but they have the assurance to affirm the absurdity. The science of geometry is understood by its professors; the science of politics is not; nor can it be understood by venal legislators or corrupt magistrates.

It may be said, who are likely to understand the science, if not those daily occupied by public business? The daily occupation may be among the reasons of their ignorance. It is the
business

business of the legislator to form laws for specified occasions; it is that of the supreme magistrate to have them executed: it is not necessary, it is not useful, that the legislator or the magistrate should be a politician, farther than to be aware of the limits of his occupation. Men of science, as I have already observed; men, in the habit of combining causes, and disentangling their operations; these alone are politicians: and no man of real science will presume to affirm, what is true in theory is false in practice; or that a theory formed on proper data, and calculated for utility or happiness, is impracticable.

That particular men may be incapable or unwilling to reduce the best theory to practice, may be allowed. That an English Parliament may see the nation verging on ruin, and not know the great or immediate cause: and that a delegated executive power, in a family recently honored with it, may drag one immense mass of the empire to oppress the other, or to desolate the whole; are facts which astonish the world, taught by romances on the Constitution, that Englishmen were free, made laws by delegates, and limited the Crown to certain duties for the good of the state. Englishmen learnt their political creeds from these romances copied into political breviaries; * and seemed intoxicated

intoxicated with the illusion, until Despair, as she suddenly opened her arms to receive them, maliciously pointed out the loss of their *political Liberty*. Nothing was heard but the confused clamor of orators and patriots, for the majesty or power of the people: but no power, no traces of majesty were to be found. Influence or venality in an intriguing court and rapacious aristocracy, had been occupied since the Revolution in building an edifice on sand; in constructing a free constitution, without political Liberty; *which is its foundation*. The winds blew; and the floods came—I will not copy the whole text—as I hope the house is not yet fallen.

I have the honor to be,

SIR,

Your sincere, and very humble servant.

March 5, 1782.

* See Blackstone's Introduction copied from Montesquieu; and De Lolme's Constitution of England copied from Blackstone.

LET-

LETTER III.

Short History of Political Liberty in England.

Il pourra arriver que la constitution sera libre, & que le citoyen ne le sera point. Le citoyen pourra être libre, & la constitution ne l'être pas. Dans ces cas, la constitution sera libre de droit, & non de fait; le citoyen sera libre de fait, & non pas de droit.

MONTESQ. Esp. de L. b. xii.

The constitution may happen to be free, but not the citizen. The citizen may be free, and not the constitution. In these cases, the constitution will be free by right, and not in fact; the citizen will be free in fact, and not by right.

SIR,

BEFORE I apply to the object of these Letters, the definitions of Political Liberty, I will give a short history of it in England, from the settlement of the Saxons to the commencement of the reign of George the Third.

When the Saxons had effected their settlement, Spelman says, they convened yearly an assembly of all the landholders of the kingdom, called Mycel-gemot, or Folkmote: and in that

that affembly, the conduct of the King and the Wittenagemot or Parliament, was fubmitted to a *revifal*. I am aware that the Wittenagemot was not an affembly of delegates.

The *Miroir de Juftices* alfo fays, the bufinefs of the Affembly of Freeholders was, " to take care the people received no wrong from the king himfelf, his queen, or their children." The king and nobles, on that occafion, were blended with the people; and were perfonally accountable for public actions. In Germany, the chief Druid prefided, to render the general or national judgement a folemn and important act of religion. In England, the honor was conferred on the king, if the deliberations were not required on his mifconduct.

The offices of the King and of the Wittenagemot being afcertained; and the freeholders of the nation having a regular method of revifing the conduct of Government, the refult was a ftate of Political Liberty.

It muft not be concealed, the proprietors of land were not numerous, compared with the prefent freeholders of England; or that farmers and tradefmen were in a condition of vaffallage. The ftate, therefore, enjoyed a high degree

degree of political, while nearly deftitute of civil Liberty. In England, thefe bleffings have not accompanied each other.

The Saxon conftitution, beautiful in its general ftructure, though defective in important parts, was fhattered by the Danes, and reftored by the immortal Alfred. It was deftroyed at the Conqueft; and fluctuating forms of tyranny continued hovering over the land; moderated by the introduction of the Commons in Parliament by Edward the Firft, by the provifions of the great charter, the humiliation of the ariftocracy by Henry the Seventh, the religious Liberty extorted by the Puritans; and by the Revolution in 1688.

But thefe events touched not a link of the chain which had fhackled political Liberty. The Commons affembled by Edward the Firft, were deputies from the king's tenants or boroughs, to fettle talliages oppreffively exacted by his officers. They conftituted no part of the legiflature; and when they gave their petitions a higher tone, on being joined by the knights of the fhires, they were regarded as innovators, or called fturdy beggars; by an executive power, and ariftocracy, which, at the fuppreffion of the Folkmote, felt all the powers of the community in their hands.

From

From the Conqueft to the Revolution, a conteft fubfifted between the fpirit of defpotifm, always haunting the throne, and a powerful ariftocracy; the Houfe of Commons being, as it remains, under the direction of the king and the nobles. The Revolution was effected by popular chiefs, happily concurring in public wifhes; who were as difinclined to a Folkmote, or a conftitutional exercife of democratic power, as the arbitrary adherents of the prince they expelled.

A new fabric was haftily formed at the Revolution; an ariftocracy, holding the Houfe of Commons in its hands, ftipulated conditions with the Crown, which had apparent tendencies to political Liberty.

If the Houfe of Commons had been freed from the influence of the King and the Lords; if it had been conftituted, a delegation from the People, though its immediate bufinefs be legiflation; it might have performed fome of the offices of a political cenfor. Being an affembly which muft continue fitting a confiderable time, among objects dangerous to the frailties of human nature, it muft have been an infufficient fubftitute for the Mycel-gemot; and could not have fecured the political Liberty of the People. But,

not

not being independent of the Prince and Aristocracy, it has been hardly any obstruction to their
pernicious views: and the History of England,
from the Revolution to this time, is merely a
history of contending factions for the direction
of the King, in the exercise of an unsatisfactory,
unprofitable, and mischievous power; while the
people have been destitute of proper means of
relief, being destitute of political Liberty.

 I am,

  S I R,

   Your most humble servant,

March 6, 1782.

LETTER IV.

View of the Administration of Government, in the Reign of George the Third, as far as the Subject is concerned.

Il pourroit être que cette nation ayant été autrefois soumise à un pouvoir arbitraire, en auroit en plusieurs occasions conservé le stile ; de maniere que, sur le fonds d'un gouvernement libre, on verroit souvent la forme d'un gouvernement absolu. Espr. des L. 19. c. 27.

This nation having formerly been subject to arbitrary power, may possibly preserve the style of it on many occasions; and in such a manner, as to let us frequently see, on the foundations of a free government, the form of an absolute power.

DEAR SIR,

SEEDS deposited at the Revolution, did not produce fruits in maturity until the reign of George the Third.

The errors blended with the Institutions of that Æra were the following; that the rights of political and civil Liberty originate in property, not in industry, talents, or virtues; that it is sufficient to the purposes of a free Constitution to render parliament a reprefentation of the property, not of the people of the country; that to prevent a repetition of the violence on Charles the Firft, a doctrine fhould be infinuated and gradually eftablifhed, that the perfon of the Lord's Anointed is facred, that the King can do no wrong, and is not accountable; that refponfibility fhould be in the King's advifer, who may be his vifir, prime minifter, cabinet council, favorite, or miftrefs.

By fubftituting the reprefentation of property, for that of men, the landholders obtained poffeffion of two important branches of the political conftitution; the power of the ancient affembly, of freeholders, and that of legiflation: and they were configned to a parliament, which, by flight manœuvres, might be free from refponfibility.

The Crown was deftined not to a conftitutional limitation, but a ftate of perpetual tutelage, under the hereditary guardianfhip of the families who had introduced the houfe of Hanover. But the claims of the truftees not being generally admitted, and an oppofition ftarting up; advantages were taken of apprehenfions for the fecurity of religion and of the reigning family, to eftablifh a principle, that to render

the

the operations of government practicable, the effect of deliberation in parliament should be taken away, and a settled majority provided in favor of the ruling Administration.

Thus a system of political despotism was involved in the complex machinery of forms: but civil jurisprudence improving, and a harmony founded on gratitude subsisting between the first princes of the House of Hanover and the great leaders of the English aristocracy, hardly any of its inconveniences were felt in some time. Fortunate circumstances in commercial adventures, and brilliant success in iniquitous wars, assisted in forming an interval of *artificial* splendor in the reign of George the Second, which astonished the world.

Previous to that interval, the plan of parliamentary influence was fixed, but its operations were not always peaceful: the constituent parts of government vibrated on delicate points; and the people, or rather the populace (for there is a material distinction in them) became of consequence by clamor and tumult. Tumults are attributed by foreign speculatists to essential defects in free governments. They have been owing in England to the imperfect structure of its political constitution; they are not more neceffary to a free government, than irregularities to the movements of an excellent machine.

Our conftitution is eftimated from the inftitutions of the Revolution; it may therefore be proper to remove fome errors to which the tranfactions of that period have given rife. For events depending wholly on the management of public paffions, and oratory being the principal inftrument in fuch management, it has been imagined the principles of Liberty require an eternal warfare; and that no man is fit for the direction of public bufinefs, who has not fpirit to direct ftorms or regulate tempefts.

The people of England perceiving they were detached from all influence on the Conftitution, while amufed with the forms of freedom, conceived a hatred of government; which is alfo erroneoufly deemed effential to the fpirit of Liberty. They formed attachments, in hopes of protection. from particular leaders. That gave rife to temporary ftratagems for popularity; which agitated the nation, under various impoftors until the talents of Mr. Pitt * effected a temporary combination of fermenting or contending principles — and, mounted on the wings of all the winds, conducted a nation, poifoned perhaps in her whole

* Afterwards Lord Chatham.

frame,

frame, to point her burſting paſſions at her enemies.

When this paroxyſm ſubſided; and Britain ſeemed wearied of victory and falſe glory; George the Third aſcended the throne of her dominions.

Among the brilliant qualities of Mr. Pitt, none were more remarkable than the facility with which he paſſed from one ſituation to another, until he ſeized the moſt advantageous. He forced himſelf into public notice, by an oppoſition to the Whigs, who held the Crown in tutelage. In the moment of victory over the miniſter, he ſeized his place; became a Whig, and the moſt deſpotic guardian the prince had ever known. This conſtituted his glory; and this brought on his diſgrace.

The young prince had pledged his power before he poſſeſſed it: but the Favorite had not the talents of Mr. Pitt; and the period of popular agitation or paſſion was nearly terminated. The manner of Lord Chatham's retreat had exaſperated the nation, which had credited his pretenſions; the great body of the *People* withdrew its attention from government; left the *Populace* to reſent the injuries, or to ſanctify the

the pretenfions, of Mr. Wilkes; and to drive the Favorite with execrations from his mafter's prefence.

The fyftem of the Prince's reign, however, had been firmly fixed; to emancipate the throne from a ftate of tutelage; to apply the produce of finance, which feemed inexhauftible, to eftablifh a decided majority in Parliament; and to make a King his own minifter, who has been folemnly declared incapable of wrong, and accountable to no power on earth.

The following doctrine, therefore, was revived in all its luftre, *Rex* eft vicarius & minifter Dei in terra: omnis quidem fub eo eft, & ipfe fub nullo; nifi tantum fub Deo.* A celebrated Commentator † paraphrafed it in the following words, which laid the foundation of his fucceeding honours—" By law the perfon of the king is facred, even though the meafures purfued in his reign be completely tyrannical and arbitrary; for no jurifdiction on earth has a power to try him in a criminal way, much lefs to condemn him to punifhment."—This is the doctrine held by the Marattas refpecting their *Rajah*; but they render it confiftent, by fhut-

---

* Bract. † Blackftone.

ing

ing him up with his women; and committing the whole government to the *Peshwa*, who affects to be responsible. The ingenious Commentator, while compiling a system of constitutional and legal knowledge for fine gentlemen, had not consulted the numerous authorities which prove the general assembly of the people have not only a right in reason, but in fact or in precedent, to revise the conduct of the king; or to sit in judgement on him; as on every delegation or assembly intrusted with power.

Readers who would rather credit Dr. Blackstone than consult those antiquated authorities, may find the purport of them collected by the late learned and candid Dr. Squire;* whose Work is better calculated to impress a just idea of the general outlines of the English Constitution than the plausible novels, which have lately obtained applause; because they flatter the vanity of the English nation, with the false opinion that it has contrived the wisest government in the world.

The doctrine was established: the King incapable of wrong, and unaccountable, became

* Squire's Essay on the Anglo-Saxon Government of England.

his own minister. The revenues of a nation, indefinitely rich, were applied to remove all obstacles in parliament. The people were reduced to a state of insignificance: and the numerous colonies annexed to the kingdom, were declared the subjects of a nation which had lost all influence in the administration of its own government; and had forgotten its political Liberty.

Slaves are for extending slavery; as disagreeable women would annihilate beauty. To the honor of the great body of the people, they abhorred the attempts of reducing the Americans beneath the rank of British subjects. But the Crown possessed the powers of government: and resistance would have been fruitless, if the empire had been compact; or if the spirit of tyranny had been equal to its design. The fools who were amused with the promises of being lords of America, would have seen the chain which had bound their fellow subjects, riveted on themselves; and despotism, gorged with the blood of virtuous citizens, would have enthroned itself in horrid majesty on the ruins of the commonwealth.

I am,
SIR,
Sincerely yours.

March 7, 1782.

LETTER V.

Views of the Conduct of Parties in Opposition to the Administration of George III. at the Time of writing these Letters.

D'autant mieux que ceux qui s'opposeroient le plus vivement à la puissance executrice, ne pouvant avouer les motifs intéressés de leur opposition, ils augmenteroient les terreurs du peuple qui ne sçauroit jamais au juste s'il seroit en danger ou non. Mais cela même contribueroit à lui faire eviter les vrais périls où il pourroit dans la suite être exposé.

L'Esprit des Loix, l. 19. c. 7.

As those who oppose the executive power with the most ardor, cannot avow the interested motives of their opposition, they heighten the terrors of the people, who can never be certain whether they are in danger, or not. But even this contributes to make them avoid real evils, to which they might otherwise have been exposed.

DEAR SIR,

LORD Chatham was a meteor, acting on public passions. While the views or interests of the aristocracy were in a state of vibration, the talents of an orator were of importance. Such passions may be biassed by eloquence: but venality is impenetrable to all arts and all confiderations. The Whig intereft, as it depended on precedent or prejudice, funk in a blaze with the factitious reputation of Lord Chatham.

Venality feemed eftablifhed; and competent to the ordinary purpofes of adminiftration, when the project was conceived, of bringing America under the arbitrary power of the Crown, through the intervention of a majority in Parliament. The Whigs, already difaffected, united in oppofition to it: and for the firft time, were inftructed, that property is not a permanent foundation of political power. Nine tenths of the property of the nation, were in the hands of men, averfe to the injury intended againft America. But arrangement, method, and power were on the fide of thofe who poffeffed the remaining tenth.

It has been affirmed of all oppofitions to government, they are actuated by interefted and factious motives. It does not appear, the gentlemen who oppofed the American War, could have had any interefts but in common with perfons of property and principle, through the empire. Factious they muft have been, as connected with parties having views on the management of public affairs. Government had long been

been the object of contending factions: it was possessed by a faction; and whenever obtained by Whigs, through parliamentary influence, it will be by a party having the properties of faction; more moderate and popular perhaps in its principles and measures; but still a faction, formed by the power or influence of chieftains, not by those of the whole people.

If experiments had been made to prove that truth, they could not have been more decisive than those afforded by the conduct of parties in the reign of George III.

With the advantages of superior property, credit, and talents, the opposition hardly ever made impressions on a disciplined phalanx, surrounding the throne; draining the country of treasures, to execute plans evidently as impracticable, as they were odious to the disposition and disgraceful to the character of the nation. Repeated disappointments or accumulated insults turned the Whig leaders to the people: who had been omitted in political arrangements for a thousand years; though constituting the basis of all legitimate power. The sudden dismemberment of of the empire; exulting eagerness in neighboring powers to seize its broken fragments; distress occasioned by the lavish expenditure of public

public money; and daily spectacles of thousands torn from their families or country; and forced with aching hearts, to strew provinces with the bodies of their friends:— these horrid objects, obtruded on high-spirited and generous minds, convulsed the land. The friends of their country—for they may be so denominated, whatever their motives, rouzed the people to assert the rights of self-preservation. But with the same effect, as if they had summoned the ocean instantly to yield rain, or to afford springs and rivulets. The previous dispositions had not been made: and the people proved an unwieldly, inactive, or useless mass. They had been accustomed to look up to Parliament for relief from the exorbitant exactions of the Crown. They were not prepared to control a Parliament, in collusion with the executive power, to extinguish every spark of political Liberty which lay scattered through the commonwealth.

Persons of influence in counties offered plans of association; from which hopes were entertained. It is with regret I speak of those plans as being hastily or crudely formed; exciting false hopes in the people, and promoting the views or interests of individuals.

Associ-

Affociations were formed, either by the sheriff fummoning the freeholders of the county and directing them to unite; or by the influence of noblemen and gentlemen over neighbors, inducing them to deliberate on the grievances of the nation. If public diftrefs had driven the majority of the people into affociations, that majority would have had no right, though it had force, to controul or correct the exceffes of the executive and legiflative powers. The other divifion of the people not having been confulted, and not under an obligation to attend the fummons given, would have reafonably complained of the fame kind of injuftice which had affociated the majority. Nothing lefs than a plan, including the whole nation, and obtaining its inclination or judgement, can give rife to the conftitutional and permanent power of the people, to prevent or correct the difpofition of the legiflature to opprefs them.

But the affociations to which I refer, not being the thoufandth part of the nation, could not difcover or exprefs its inclination; they were formed on the fpot, by the perfons affembled; not by the inhabitants of the town or diftrict they affected to reprefent. Any iniquitous powers might be produced on fuch principles; which appeared to me at all times to have no tendency

dency to political Liberty. It is true, refolutions were formed, and petitions drawn up, which were afterwards communicated to thousands, and signed; but the order of things was inverted. The sentiments and inclinations of individuals or of small assemblies, were forced downwards into the mass of the people; an unnatural, ineffectual mode of operation. Delegated powers should proceed upwards from the people; in the English projects of reformation, they were imputed to them by ambitious leaders, or arbitrary combinations of political Apostles.

The gradual rise of these associations, Government considered with contempt; and the country with mingled hope and pity. They proceeded in their measures with indecision or timidity, distrusting the ground they were upon: the possible consequences of their assemblies were exhibited in horrid characters, in the fate of the Protestant Association: and there is but one general opinion concerning them,—they will silently crumble into oblivion.

The interposition of the City of London may have different effects; because the city of London possesses power. A corporation founded on the iniquitous principles of monopoly, remonstrating

monstrating in the cause of Liberty, like a tyger in the cause of mercy, is a suspicious phenomenon. It is true the strides of power have been so rapid as to alarm those chiefs of parties, and members of corporations, who were content with the exercise as well as the fruits of *moderate oppression*.

If circumstances were wanting to prove the measures of the different parties not properly taken, they would be found in their disagreement and discord. Actuated by a common principle, they could not agree on what they wanted. Constituents were applied to; and then insulted with declarations, that their delegates were responsible only to the whole empire. In short, this region of the political world became a chaos of discordant opinions; into which good men looked with despair; and the nation might have lost its senses, if it had not been hushed by the irresistible pressure of half the world menacing sudden ruin, for the folly and iniquity of the American War.

When I first conceived the design of these Letters, I determined to confine myself to England. But the proceedings of the Irish volunteers,

teers, being adduced as objections to my general principles, I cannot omit them.

The condition of the Roman Catholics in Ireland, is reproachful to the humanity and understanding of Government; and will prevent for ages, the acquisition of freedom.— If we suppose the Roman Catholics not in existence, or in a state of slavery; and the Protestants the only free inhabitants of the island; they have acted apparently on right principles, in arming themselves, electing officers, and forming provinces into regiments commanded by chieftains. But their plan is defective: any protestants may be volunteers who can arm, or find leisure to attend the days of discipline. Those who have not the inclination or ability, may decline the trouble. The greater part will decline: and disciplined volunteers will assume the political power. It is probable, whole provinces may be wearied by military duties, while others persevere; until, by discipline, and the instigation of ambitious leaders, they command the destiny of the nation. Regulations, defective in essential principles, produce numerous and fatal inconveniences.

It may be alledged, resistances in America were made by partial associations. The follies

of

of the English administration accumulated so suddenly, and to such unexampled degrees of enormity, that the natives of the Colonies were at once roused; and they gave authority to associations which would otherwise have been ineffectual.

There are situations; such as those of Ireland and America; in which it is imprudence to neglect measures, because they are not unexceptionable, or the best to be imagined. They presented urgent and critical moments; in which all bodies have dispensing powers. I wish to guard against the custom of blending expedients with principles; or forming such systems of chicane as those which disgrace the general policy of Europe.

Associations in England were formed in alarming, but not in critical circumstances: they had been years in contemplation; and to ensure success,* in a period so enlightened they should

* The general corruption of the times is a fruitful source of declamation, when dangers or miseries disturb the public tranquillity. What had the great body of the people of England to do with the follies or absurdities of the American war? No period of our history can be pointed out, in which so many private virtues were exercised, as that which has been dishonoured by its unfortunate events: the industry that supported its expence, removes all imputations on the character of the people.

D   have

have rested on clear and scientific data. The friend of these associations were misled, by America and Ireland, into a conclusion, that they proceeded on universal and infallible principles. Success is a precarious proof of truth: and the persons who led divisions of the people into deliberate or important measures, should have studied the science, whose principles they meant to apply.

I am, SIR,

    Your most humble servant,

March 8, 1782.

While these Letters were in the press, the measures of the American war were reprobated by a vote of the House of Commons. It was carried, on the supposition that success and disappointment are the tests of right and wrong. By the success of Gen. Conway's motion; and on the assurance that America would not treat with the authors of its calamities; their places

were

were assigned to the leaders of opposition. That measures more popular and useful will be pursued, cannot be doubted: for the continuance of the administration a single month, depends on them. But the change, though relieving us from instant distresses and apprehensions, does not promise any remedy for their causes. The expedients of patronage and family interference are as fatal to Liberty as the influence of the Crown.

If flight or artful palliatives are to be administered: if the extremities only are to be trimmed, to shew the address of the operators; while the disorder silently and gradually consumes us; we shall regret the ministry of Lord North was not continued in its career of absurdities: in the extremity of distress, we should either have suddenly perished, or sought the means to recover vigor and health. What Mr. Locke says of good princes, may be applied to popular administrations; by obtaining extraordinary confidence and power, they furnish claims or precedents for successors, which are asserted to injurious and fatal purposes. If Augustus had not been beloved, Tiberius, Nero, and Caligula, would not have sported with the lives of the Romans. If the Whigs, who effected the Revolution in 1688, had not been implicitly confided in, and assumed unconstitutional powers; the late contemptible administration, could not have involved us in an absurd and disgraceful war. The gentlemen who hold the reins of government, owe us some atonement for the errors of their ancestors.

April 15, 1782.

LETTER VI.

The Method of introducing, establishing, or recovering a State of Political Liberty.

Que si les disputes etoient formées à l' occasion de la violation des loix fondamentales, & qu'une puissance étrangere parut; il y auroit une révolution qui ne changeroit pas le forme du gouvernement, ni sa constitution: car les révolutions que forme la Liberté ne sont qu'une confirmation de la Liberté.
L' Esprit des Loix, l. xix. c. 27.

But if the disputes arise from the violation of fundamental laws; and a foreign power appear; a revolution would take place, which would alter neither the form of government nor the constitution: for revolutions which are formed by Liberty, are only confirmations of that Liberty.

DEAR SIR,

IF I have accomplished my purpose in the Letters already written; it is evident the Constitution of England, whatever panegyrics have been bestowed on it, is unfinished and incomplete. The Saxons possessed political Liberty, by reserving the supreme power in the people: but they held labor, industry, and the arts, in slavery; and the administration of justice at the pleasure of individuals. They were therefore destitute of civil Liberty. At the Revolution in 1688, provisions and arrangements introduced a high state of civil, while they have nearly suppressed political Liberty.

This accounts for jealousies, apprehensions, factions, or tumults often endangering the State; which negligent observers attribute to the nature, not the defects, of the English Constitution. In providing for civil, not for political Liberty, we have preferred the lesser to the greater blessing. The peace and security of the people, from the power of self-preservation, and the capacity of repelling encroachments of government, are of much superior importance to any private advantages, from the administration of justice to individuals. Indeed the latter cannot be enjoyed in a high degree; or long subsist, without the former. This may be seen in the attempts of the wisest Roman emperors to preserve civil, after the expiration of political Liberty. The system of jurisprudence formed on their edicts, is ingenious and benevolent; but the senate (the Roman Parliament) was in a state of servile dependence on the imperial diadem: the people were out of the political balance; and the empire was convulsed with misery, or enjoyed peace,

peace, as the Prince chanced to be a philofopher, an ideot, or a tyrant.

It is the condition of political infecurity, from perfidy in its pretended reprefentatives, or ambition in the Crown, which gives the people of England that air of perpetual difcontent; that impatience of authority; that infolence to fuperiors; apparently ungrateful and brutal, in perfons furrounded with bleffings. But the people feel with more truth, than fpeculatifts reafon. Perceiving evident collufions of the legiflative and executive powers; that they have no mode of diffolving them without infurrections; that laws are obtained, or burdens accumulated, under fallacious forms, to a degree of enormity which would coft a fultan his head: they cherifh a conftant fufpicion or hatred of government. No fpecies of defpotifm can be fo dreadful, as that of a free Conftitution half-formed; when all its abufes affume the authority of eftablifhments. This is nearly the cafe in England: and the neighboring ftates, who have never tafted Liberty, afford an afylum to thoufands of its oppreffed and emigrating inhabitants.

The tyranny of a fingle man is circumfcribed by a fmall fphere, and beyond it all is peace.

Cuftoms check caprice; and privileges are inviolate. But a political Conftitution imperfectly conftructed, and corrupted by venality, will carry its abufes to an incredible extent: it would refine upon the artifices of the wily defpots of Turkey or Hindoftan.

It is faid, there can be no remedy in fuch cafes, efpecially if the country be of great extent, or the people numerous. Political Liberty may be enjoyed in fmall ftates; becaufe the people may affemble, to keep the fenate and magiftrates within proper bounds. In Crete; which furnifhed the model of ancient republics; the people had recourfe to occafional infurrections, to ftimulate the indolence, or check the ambition of the magiftrate: as nature has recourfe to tempefts, to purify or animate the elements. But thefe expedients cannot take place in large and populous nations, without perpetual anarchy.

It is the ufual artifice of fophifts, to confider a fubject only in one point of view. Few men will argue from the ufe of popular infurrections in Crete, to the expedience of them in France or in England; where the people could not move, but in extenfive and ruinous inundations.

If multitudes were collected at random, and every man were moderate and wife as Newton,

the

the whole might act with folly or violence: becaufe low and violent paffions only can be inftantly diffufed, or agitate large affemblies.

As an animal is fufceptible of life, only when his parts are in certain arrangements, not when he is of any determinate fize; fo the mafs or body of the people is rendered capable of fenfibility, paffion, or judgment, by the mode of arranging its parts; not by their number. Small numbers, by admitting a free and intimate circulation of thoughts, are fufceptible of judgement. Large numbers, by admitting only the impulfe of ftrong or common emotions on all their parts, are fufceptible of paffion only; and cannot form judgements, whatever be the abilities of individuals: very numerous multitudes, like immenfe maffes of matter, are void even of general feeling.

Multitudes, like matter, muft be arranged; muft be organifed: and they may be, in any quantities, or to any extent. The nature of their fenfibility, paffion, or judgment, will depend on arrangement or organifation. An elephant is a continent of organifed matter; compared with the little animal, that directs his family, and affociates with his community, in a drop of water.

Any

Any numbers of men may be arranged, to form general judgements: without forcing individuals out of their situations, or producing the tumults and dangers, which attend the assemblies even of small democracies. The disposition and management of an army, will illustrate this problem. Every thing is felt with truth and rapidity, by a whole army; because it is divided into parts, connected by a gradation of officers; which are the nerves, arteries, and ligaments, of the artificial body. One of the most experienced and intelligent officers of the present age,* rests the fate of an engagement on the passions or opinions of the common soldiers in regard to their officers: and though they have no influence on the appointment of a general; he affirms, that in order to ensure success, the General should be in all respects such a man as the common soldiers *would have chosen*.

I mention the army; not to recommend military government; but to shew, that division and arrangement in small connected parties, will render any numbers capable of judgement, will, or power. If the manner of forming ligaments of military union, or organs of military sensibility and judgement, were inverted; the army

* General Lloyd.

would

would exhibit the model of a people in a state to assert and enjoy the highest degree of Political Liberty. If the inferior officers were chosen by the smaller divisions of the soldiers; and those officers chose the next in rank, until the process terminated in a general: the army would represent a people in a condition to form judgements; to have will; to delegate legislative and executive powers, free and uncontrouled within certain limits, but checked, corrected, or annihilated, when, passing those limits, they oppressed or injured the community they were intended to serve.

This truth is founded on principles as clear and indisputable as any in geometry.

Geometrical definitions are admitted, because none can be substituted for them: political definitions must have the same claim, to become the permanent principles of useful science.

No definition of useful government can be substituted for, " The art of governing all, by all." It is one of the data which cannot be controverted. The difficulty has been, to arrange numerous multitudes into regular or animated bodies; which might move or act without disorder. The manner of effecting the arrangement

ment has been shewn. But as the power of the lever, and the most useful truths of mechanics, were incredible speculations; until applied to specific purposes: it is happy we can have recourse to history; and prove from experience, these principles may be applied to produce and preserve political Liberty.

Without repeating the observations already made on the Mycel-gemot, or Folkmote; we will attend to the revival of the Saxon institutions by Alfred.

Spelman says, the counties were divided into tythings or laths; who chose tything-men as representatives, in the court of the hundred; which had representatives in the county-court:—that appeals lay from tythings to hundreds; from hundreds to counties; from counties, in some cases, to the king and his barons, council, or parliament; in others, to the Folkmote or assembly of all the land-holders of the nation:—that every housholder was answerable for his wife, and those children who were under the age of fifteen; his servants, and dependents: the tything answerable for its housholders; the hundred for the tythings; the county for the hundreds. The nobility were obliged to attend

the

the court of the hundred: as the reprefentatives of particular tythings.

Thefe arrangements were probably for the purpofes of police; and they are the moft excellent which have ever been introduced. They were calculated to draw the whole force of the nation, to repel the invafions of the Danes. Whatever reafons may be imagined for them, they gave the mafs of the people an univerfal and inftantaneous *fenfibility* to all important events; enabled them to *judge*, and to *act*, without tumult, when occafion required the exertion of the whole nation.

Thefe regulations point out methods of reftoring the balance of power in the Englifh Conftitution.

But as parifhes and counties are unequal divifions; and the moft important members of the community are, not the mere poffeffors of lands, but perfons whofe induftry or talents increafe and multiply their original value; regard fhould be had to men, not to poffeffions: and they fhould be divided by their numbers, not by the fpace of ground they may happen to occupy.

Ten

Ten men, whether freeholders, tenants, housholders, or lodgers, who live on their fortune, industry, or talents; and whose habitations are contiguous, should form a tything; and elect a representative to convey the sense and opinion of his constituents, to a meeting of the representatives of ten neighbouring tythings, called a hundred; where one should be chosen to meet the representatives of the ten adjoining hundreds; and in the same manner of thousands, ten thousands, hundred thousands; until every million of the inhabitants or citizens, be represented by one. If we suppose the English nation to consist of two millions of the species of inhabitants above described; the business of the universal representation would be done in London by two persons; who would on all occasions accurately ascertain the general *inclination* and *judgement* of the nation. All the representatives should have their expences defrayed by their constituents.

To answer the purposes of these regulations; and to frustrate the attempts of the Crown to corrupt such representations; all the elections should be on the same day, and only for a year: and all the deputies be *representatives*; whose election should be void, on their departure in the slightest degree from the judgement of their

consti-

constituents. For the design of the arrangement being to obtain the sense of the people, whatever it be, and not the opinions of their deputies; no latitude should be given to representatives; who ought to decline the appointment, on differences of opinions with their constituents. All the delegates being *representatives*, who could not be otherwise employed than in supporting the public judgement; in order to influence them by corruption, the whole people must be bought.—No contest or litigation would arise from the interfering opinions or interests of the several divisions; as in all cases the minority must acquiesce, and join in enforcing the public inclination.

I wish you to observe, the first object of these letters is not to specify the necessary regulations for an adequate representation in Parliament: but to give security to the whole state against the breaches of trust, or collusions with the executive power, by which *parliaments* have often reduced the whole nation to distress. All powers, in free countries, should be checked or limited by the power of the people; regularly and fairly obtained. But the precise boundaries of these powers, or the mode of forming them, cannot be included in my present design. I am laying, or rather restoring, the

foun-

foundation—all the neceffary ftructures may be eafily erected.

It will be faid, the revival of this mode of eftablifhing political Liberty would have all the effect of innovation; and innovations, on the moft perfect principles, are hurtful, becaufe they prefs on the prejudices of the people.

This is the fhallow pretence of political jefuitifm. The throne is daily innovating; while every ftep preffes out the blood of induftry or of merit. A ftanding army is an innovation, againft the prepoffeffions, habits, and judgement, of every independent man in the nation: yet it has been eftablifhed. Is it to be imagined, the people will object to the very little trouble attending fuch arrangements, as will afford them fecurity againft the encroachments of the Crown, or the depredations of fluctuating parties in the Legiflature, plundering them in fucceffion? If they were to arm themfelves flightly, they would have a police on the beft footing; and be perfectly fecured againft the collufions of thieves and thief-takers, watchmen, conftables, churchwardens, overfeers, veftry-clerks, trading juftices, and all the expenfive appendages to the fcience of robbery.

It will be asked—in what manner can this plan be entered upon? The executive power will exert its influence against it: and the leaders of the several divisions of popular parties will attempt to discredit all arrangements, in which they may not take the command; or by which they may be blended with the people.

In June, 1780, the daring violence of a few desperadoes shewed the state of civil Government to be so feeble, that every man felt the necessity of assuming his station; or acquiring the power of defending himself and family. A disposition to associate generally prevailed: but no method was pointed out, not incumbered with military discipline; or consistent with the common occupations of peaceful citizens. Administration saw the perplexity; and improved the advantages it afforded, with a dexterity which might have been better exerted against the enemies, than the people, of the country. They encouraged military associations, knowing they would be burthensome or impracticable; but embarrassed attempts of neighborhoods to establish an easy and general police. I will mention an instance; in order to point out the treatment which the emissaries of power should always receive on such occasions.

The inhabitants of a parish in Westminster, having felt the inconvenience of military forms, wished to associate in independent parties, for the protection of their families; and they were assembled on some occasion that related to their design, when to their great astonishment, a clergyman and a magistrate entered the room. The first said, he was the rector of the parish; and the other, he was a justice of the peace: it was signified, they were commissioned from high authority to warn the assembly against doing any thing illegal. One of the company thanked them; as spies are usually thanked: and they were requested to walk out.

The creatures of the Crown, however wide it may have diffused its contagion, can form but a small body, compared with the whole nation; and cannot obstruct its designs. They succeed by arrangement or discipline: and it is our object to give similar advantages to the people.

As to the leaders of parties, their operations may be more perplexing. But talents, superior to those of intrigue and declamation, would be drawn out on the plan here recommended: men of real wisdom and merit, if there be any among these leaders, would have chances of gratifying their

their ambition, in the moſt pleaſing and honorable manner, by the election of the people; the degrading or levelling principles of common democracies could not be introduced; the utmoſt variety of characters and diſtinctions would take place: yet all orders would be impreſſed by a political neceſſity of obeying and executing the public will.

That men in general will be cautious of embarking in this neceſſary and important deſign, I can eaſily imagine. The nation has been extremely ſhy of aſſociations; though invited by men of rank, fortune, and power. But all ſteps towards arranging the people, or reviving the whole maſs into a political body, will be like the returning ſymptoms of life, attended with aſſured hopes, and irreſiſtible confidence.

It is in the power of any man of public ſpirit and honeſty, to begin the important buſineſs, who can induce a ſingle pariſh to inſtitute and regulate its police, on the principles already pointed out. The immediate conſequence of the improvement, would be clearing that pariſh of vagrants, beggars, and all thoſe uſeleſs or pernicious wretches who daily heighten the enormity of poor rates. Theſe, paſſing into other pariſhes, would put them under the neceſſity of having recourfe to fimilar meafures. And when the people were arranged for one purpofe, they would be, *for all the purpofes of political Liberty.* If individuals refrain from motives of timidity, or the influence of power; no force fhould be applied: they would fee their fellow-citizens in peaceful enjoyment of the moft effential bleffings of human fociety; while they were funk into the clafs of dependents, and vagrants; or contemned by the community as deftitute of the fpirit and privileges of citizens.

Perhaps, there is no part of the kingdom, where this plan of police might be introduced fo eafily, as in Weftminfter. If the gentlemen who affect to have the interefts of the people at heart, would employ their influence in introducing fuch arrangements, inftead of affembling and haranguing an idle or profligate populace; by producing permanent and general bleffings, they would lay the foundation of everlafting fame: and perhaps might find themfelves in the direct road to honors or emoluments.

That fuch regulations of police, would have confequences fatal to illegitimate power, was immediately perceived by Adminiftration; though not by the friends of the people, when the mob in June, 1780, held up to the world the horrid truth "that the civil liberties of England rested ultimately on an army, composed of the refuse of the land, and depending on the will of the prince." The nation seemed aghast! and, if among its senators, there had been a real and intelligent patriot, he would have directed the people, to secure their civil, by assuming their political Liberty. They saw the necessity, that every free man should be in a condition to support the magistrate when recoiling from his duty; or to defend his family from violence and extirpation, without sending to the prince for a soldier; that some bonds should unite neighborhoods, and districts, from such inundations of villainy, as must occasionally arise in communities, whose fate depends on the accidental prevalence or discomfiture of factions.

In that alarming situation, when the spirits of men were bent on inquiries, no method was put in practice, which did not rest our safety ultimately on the Crown; or on the caprice of men of fortunes in their several neighborhoods. If the people had been directed and assisted in the first privilege or duty of human society, the power of defending their families, without enlisting as soldiers; the arrangements necessary for the purpose, into tythings, hundreds, &c. would have

have introduced that universal *sensibility* which is the foundation of political Liberty.

It will be alledged (and I wish to meet all objections) that so much power in the people, would be abused; and no government can long exist under the capricious exercise of it.

If the following maxim were withdrawn, almost all the governments in Europe would crumble or disappear, ' In order to have your ' interests properly guarded, entrust them to ' others; never to yourselves.'

That the great body of the people; on whose labor, industry, and talents, the whole state depends.—I speak not of the populace, the dregs of vicious governments, who usually assemble in mobs—that the PEOPLE properly arranged; organised into sensibility, general sympathy or judgment; having the strongest and best principles of self-preservation,—should be incapable of acting on them—is an impossible supposition. It is warranted by no presumption or fact in the history of mankind. For whenever the people, in possession of political Liberty, have acted on fixed principles and regulations, (as in the best periods of the Saxon government) —it has been, with wisdom and moderation.

No

No traces of caprice, or folly can be found in their conduct. In Sparta and Rome, before the original inftitutions were deranged, the popular power was always the laft or moft reluctant in violating the political compact.

If that had not been the cafe, my claims to attention would not have been invalidated. I am not pleading for the legiflative or executive powers, which were executed by the people of ancient democracies in large affemblies:—thofe powers, when once appointed, for certain times, or within ftipulated boundaries, fhould be perfectly uncontrouled; but the people fhould have regular and effectual methods of exerting the force of the whole community (which can be only in them) to prevent abufes, or to check encroachments on thofe limits. If difcipline, principles, and fcience, are to be beftowed on a rabble to form it into an army; which is generally employed to increafe the miferies of mankind;—this certainly fhould be the cafe, in the difpofition of a people to exercife political power, on which its civil Government muft reft, if it ever reft fecurely; without which all the bleffings of human fociety muft be tinged with jealoufies, apprehenfions, and uncertainties.

If, in these Letters, I have given hints which may induce you to employ your thoughts on the subject of them; or to exert your influence, to restore to England what it has so long lost; what is so necessary to retrieve its degraded character; to unite the broken parts of its commonwealth; and to give permanency to the civil and commercial privileges it enjoys; my end will be answered. I wish to be concealed as the Author; for reasons very obvious, in the present state of political literature. On any other occasion, I should be happy in subscribing my name; and acknowledging the esteem, with which

I am,

SIR,

Your obliged, and most humble servant.

March 12, 1782.

LETTER VII.

Plan of equal Representation.

Societas nostra lapidum fornicationi simillima est, quæ casura nisi invicem obstarent; hoc ipso sustinetur.
                                             SENEC. Ep.

Society resembles an arch; which is supported by the reciprocal resistance of the stones that compose it.

DEAR SIR,

IN the preceding Letters on Political Liberty, I have shewn the democratic power, in the English Constitution, is become merely nominal: and that aristocratic factions, sometimes on moderate, sometimes on violent principles, have usurped the Government.

Every thing in nature is done by action and re-action. All powers, have resisting powers; and the whole universe is probably balanced, by combinations of opposite forces. In human institutions, the same contrivance is always attempted. The mechanic, who constructs the most simple machine; and the politician, who arranges the principles of the State, differ only
in

in the magnitude and variety of their objects. The same general laws must govern their inventions.

As the derangement of machines is owing to the improper prevalence of constituent powers: in a state, all inconveniencies or injuries are to be ascribed to the want of counter-action and resistance in some parts, to balance the pressure of others; or to assist in producing the general effect.

The magnitude of these parts; and the uncommon efforts of genius requisite to combine them, are the reasons, that human societies continue reproachful to human reason. Perhaps practical politicians, the agents or workmen in these edifices, contribute not a little to the establishment of abuses. They are occupied on parts, from which it may be impracticable to view the whole: or they have generally an interest in abuses. In every state, where it may be an object to improve and perfect the Constitution, there should be an order of men, who might add to general knowledge of business, profound and deliberate speculation; and be guardians of the state, without having an interest in its official departments.

In conftitutions, pretending to liberty, we find this general truth exemplified. Delegated powers affume the tone of tyranny, when the people cannot readily control them: and the people become capricious, violent, or defpotic, where they affemble in multitudes; and annihilate the authority of their deputies.

Every thing, in the compafs of imagination, is poffible, by method or arrangement.

In the preceding Letters, I have pointed out the mode of giving fenfibility and judgment to any number of people; to put it in their power, to balance the legiflative and executive forces of the ftate; and to put it out of their power, to become tumultuous or capricious in their exertions.

No problem in politics has ever occurred to my imagination, which I cannot folve on thefe principles, to my entire fatisfaction: and they have occupied my mind many years.

This may be an apology for my prefumption in fo readily complying with your requeft; and engaging *, in fo little time, to delineate a

* This Letter was not in the Author's firft defign.

plan

plan on a subject which has long exercised the first abilities of the nation.

The imperfections of the present House of Commons, are the following:

It would represent certain quantities of soil; and not the people, whose talents are to give it value. Or, where it pretends to represent men, as in corporations, &c. it makes a part equal to the whole. That has given rise to the extravagant idea of virtual representation; by which Colonies and Provinces are held in bondage.

The members, once seated, assume, each to to himself, a perfect independence; and claim the right of acting, not on the views or inclinations of their constituents, but on their own. All just ideas of representation are therefore lost.

The House of Commons, if it were a delegation from the people, would not have a power of voting itself independent and continuing its sessions, at pleasure, or by collusions with the other branches of government. This is a stewardship totally annihilating the power of the lord; and rendering the English parliament the most absurd institution in the world.

In

In order to have the people reprefented, and not the land; to have their *fenfe, inclination,* or *judgement* expreffed and enforced by the abilities of their *actual reprefentatives*; they muft be arranged, nearly as I have pointed out in the preceding Letters: where the immediate object is, not a reprefentation for the purpofe of a legiflature; but to form political powers in the body of the people, to controul, balance, or give ftability to the legiflature and crown; and to effect the purpofes of defenfive and internal police. The want of this political power, was felt in the republics of Greece and Rome; it was not fupplied either by the Ephori or the Tribunes of the people.

A Houfe of Commons, deliberating on fupplies, and the formation of laws, fhould be an affembly of perfons actually refiding in the feveral districts of the kingdom; informed in their peculiar interefts; and able to reconcile thofe interefts with the general good.

The Houfe of Commons fhould not be fo numerous as at this time. Becaufe the larger the multitude, the lower or more contemptible the paffions, which actuate it by the mere effect of debate or eloquence. In an affembly of five hundred; men of the firft genius and merit
are

are seldom heard; tumultuous or ambitious leaders, of slender but brilliant talents, always give the law.

Whatever be the number of parliamentary members—the whole Commonwealth, however its parts may be separated, should be divided into districts; each district containing an equal number of inhabitants.

All men at the age of eighteen, not vagabonds or in the hand of justice, have a right to vote; because they contribute by their industry to the support of the state. I have had doubts concerning menial servants; on account of their dependence on masters: but the injustice of excluding them, would produce greater inconveniences, than the trouble of preventing the ill effects of that dependence.

These districts would contain too great a number of people to be brought together, and rendered susceptible of any impressions beyond those of clamour or tumult. They must be therefore arranged; as in the preceding letter. Ten adjoining inhabitants to choose by ballot an *actual representative*; who, with the ten representatives of adjoining tythings, should chuse an *actual representative* of a hundred; and in the same man-

manner of thousands, &c. until the choice of the district center in one, who may represent it in Parliament. All the processes to be on the same day; and the expences of representation, in all its gradations, to be defrayed by the constituents.

The very essence of the plan is, that the judgment of the people be expressed by the delegate; and that the Parliament be a *representation*, in the strict or severe sense of the word. This is necessary, because there is no general principle of government which can be substituted for the judgment or will of the people; for if right, it draws with it the whole power of the community; if wrong, it is corrected by the necessary principle of self-preservation.

The obligation of representatives to exercise their abilities, wholly on the subservience of the interests of their constituents to those of the state, will render it useless in the Crown to attempt corrupting them; if the Crown should be at liberty to misemploy the public treasure in that manner. For the delegate being bound to a strict representation; the constituents must be bought, to obtain the voice of the representative.

The

The mifchiefs of the Englifh government have arifen from a difunion of its feveral parts, under the idea, of reciprocal independence. As in the human body, the functions of each member, are perfectly unembarraffed, though it be united to the body, and fubject to its general ftrength : fo in a political ftate, the deliberative and executive parts are free or independent, in their particular exertions, though annexed to the general body ; and bound to it, by fuch ligaments as render them fubfervient to its collective force.

The members of the Englifh Parliament, might be united to the body of the people, by the arrangement I have pointed out ; be perfectly free within the limits of their duty; but liable to immediate checks or reftraints on paffing thofe limits. The fenfe of the diftrict, on the conduct of a member, would be fo eafily taken in this method, that no deviation in his conduct, would probably be overlooked.

It is unneceffary to fay, if the people were once in poffeffion of a mode of acting regularly and eafily as a political body, that Parliaments would be of fhorter duration than at prefent ;*
that

---

* All thefe circumftances muft be left to the determination of the people. It is truly ridiculous to obferve the contentions

that they would meet at stated times; and adjourn themselves, within the limits of their political existence, on the conclusion of the business before them: that such an assembly would not attempt an atrocious breach of trust in voting itself intitled to long or numerous sessions; and that the Crown, forced within its boundaries, would be better employed in its various and important offices, than in attempting to mislead or embarrass operations, under the controul or correction of a general and well-directed principle of self-preservation in the whole nation.

The assembly being formed; the deliberative business should always originate in small committees. I should wish them not to consist of more than ten or twelve persons; because in all my life, I have not known a larger assembly, capable of forming wise or good determinations.

On the first step taken in a committee, the business should be published: not only for the information of the house; but of all the people,

tions of parliamentary projectors, on these points; where all opinions are impertinent if meant for more than information. An act of the legislature has no real authority in such cases; much less the opinion of a member of parliament.

For this and other purposes, of equal importance, the press should be perfectly free: it is the only vehicle of general information; and without it a people can neither be virtuous nor happy: restraints on it are the sole causes of the abuses by which it is disgraced.

The business being digested in the committee, it should be proposed to the whole house; and determined by a majority.

If we suppose the committee, to have arranged matters with wisdom; it is extremely probable that a numerous assembly would reject those arrangements, for a numerous assembly seems unsusceptible of wisdom; the house of Commons should therefore be greatly reduced in its number, unless it deliberate in classes, and give votes as the tribes did at Rome, or as juries do in England, by the deputy of every class.*

We

---

* There are no objections to plans of this nature for an equal representation; unless it be those which arise from corrupt or selfish motives. Wherever private property (even in infamous boroughs) is to be sacrificed; the actual proprietors should receive full compensation. The expence attending its would hardly amount to the sum expended at every election, in diffusing perjury and all kinds of immorality through the land. The scheme of the turnpike roads

(a tri-

We are now at such a distance from every idea of wisdom or goodness, in political concerns, that I suppose this plan, simple and practicable as it is, will be ranked among the speculative visions which are stored for better or more enlightened times.

In all the sciences, men are young: in the science of government, they are children.—— Ants, and bees, and beavers, exhibit institutions, which reproach the best forms of government on earth. We herd at random; or are driven by miscreants of our species, in a manner, to which the most dastardly animal would not submit: a flock of sheep would not be driven to slaughter, by one of its own kind.

If an attempt to state the first principles of human policy; or to apply them to the present disgraceful condition of the Liberty and legislature of my country, should prove wholly fruitless, in regard to the public, I shall submit to the disappointment; in common with thousands; whose thoughts are probably occupied in the same manner.

(a trifling object compared with that before us) was not impeded by the necessity of much greater and more inconvenient incroachments on the property of individuals.

I shall have a pleasure, however, in having obeyed your commands: as I should always in shewing the esteem with which I have the honor to be.

SIR

Your obliged, and

Most humble servant

THE AUTHOR.

March 15, 1782.

ON the publication of the preceding Letters, the author was invited to assist in the general efforts for a reform of Parliament. Those efforts were understood by Government, as the artifices of political partizans, to obtain situations of power or emolument. The author was not so well informed; and he reluctantly admitted a similar conviction, when he had attentively compared the professions and conduct of popular impostors.

TO THE

ASSOCIATED CORRESPONDENTS

Of a Periodical Paper, called,

THE FRIEND OF THE PEOPLE.

GENTLEMEN,

THE Proposals you have distributed, are on a plan so excellent, that I would shew my approbation, in the only method in my power; by occasionally sending you a Paper.

I wrote the following letter to Lord Surrey,* in the month of February. The subject being of consequence to the nation; and the letter written according to my best skill and information, I think it a duty to lay it before the Public: and I beg it may be, in your Paper.

I would offer myself a member, if I had not deliberately resolved, not to entangle myself with the plans or opinions of Societies; and my

* Afterwards Duke of Norfolk

health and engagements did not render additional obligations or duties impracticable. I will send you an essay when I can: and you may insert, or return it as you please.

I am, Gentlemen,

A Volunteer, warmly in the Interests of
THE PEOPLE.

Tuesday April 1, 1783.

*** We shall be very happy in this Gentleman's correspondence. He will observe, that we have taken the liberty to make some slight alterations where his observations pressed too pointedly on Associations, Committees, and Societies, for whose views and intentions we have so much respect. His Plan is bold, and well imagined; and his manner of stating it liberal and manly. Those who think that benefits must descend to the People, and not ascend from them, will differ with him in opinion: and we shall insert *their* various schemes with pleasure. A reform of abuses, and an *equal Representation of the People*, are the first objects of our Paper. If the present writer should have failed, some person among our correspondents may be so happy as to point out *the Method* by which these ends may be obtained. In the mean time we think it neceffary to apprize our readers, that their time fhall not be wafted in mere controverfies and perfonalities. Bad meafures may be arraigned; and bad men expofed: but it will be on account of the Public; and not to harrafs Adminiftrations, or to injure private characters.

TO THE RIGHT HONORABLE

EARL of SURRY.

My Lord,

I HAVE attended to your Lordfhip's conduct, refpecting the Reprefentation of the People, with fome care: and if I were not of opinion, you poffefs more integrity or public principle, than moft of thofe who undertake, or wifh to undertake public bufinefs, I would not give *you* or *myfelf*, the trouble of this letter.

If I were to profefs difintereftednefs, and love of my country, as my only motives—they are profeffions fo proftituted, as to be infamous; and I might be in danger of being deemed an impoftor. No man can be difinterefted in a state of things analagous to a general wreck: he must have something to hope, or something to apprehend; and, perhaps, the best sentiment which can be felt for the political situation of this country is, *Compassion inclining to contempt.*

It is supposed the evils that have sunk England into its present dishonor, originated in the House of Commons: which has not been a Representation of the people; and has been often and easily corrupted to effect purposes of the most flagitious nature. Burthens, oppressions, and misfortunes, in the obstinate persecution of an infamous war, have roused respectable bodies in several parts of the kingdom, to attempt the removal of the evil.

It is to point out circumstances which embarrass the attempts; and may render them abortive or of inconsiderable effect, that I address your Lordship.

These bodies are called committees of Counties or Districts; where, I apprehend, they have not been *chosen* by majorities of the inhabitants: and they record *Resolutions,* when it would be adviseable to *offer modest opinions.* I extend the observation, to societies in London, which seem to be respectable. They are not, I am sorry they

they are not, deputations, with certain diſtricts pledged for their ſupport. I am therefore apprehenſive, their diſcuſſions can only produce the opinions of individuals who form or who influence the Societies; not reſolutions carrying with them the ſlighteſt authority.

Will not theſe be felt, on trial, to be eſſential defects in ſuch bodies? And if their conſtitutions muſt not be changed, could not their language be moderated, as well from a regard to truth, as to prudence or decorum?

If theſe bodies were admitted to be delegations, with competent authority; their proceedings would not appear directed by that wiſdom to be expected from their members. This may be owing to the cuſtom of doing buſineſs, by orations; the worſt mode to obtain wiſe or good reſolutions.

But waving ſuch important defects, and allowing the Societies to be on a footing with the inhabitants of thoſe Boroughs which have lately applied to parliament; on what pretence of wiſdom, uſefulneſs, or practicability can the *Houſe of Commons* be petitioned? Either it is, a proper and adequate repreſentation; or it is not. If adequate, why diſturb it? If not, its acts, even

within

within its province, muſt be nullities. Why is that province to be enlarged? Why is the unconſtitutional dominion of Parliament to be extended at the expence of the political Liberty of the Community?—If it be a fair delegation, entruſted with powers for particular purpoſes—ſurely thoſe who delegate, not the perſons delegated, ſhould aſcertain the conditions of the truſt, or the manner of executing it. If it be an unconſtitutional Aſſembly, it muſt be owing to ſome irregularity, ſome fault, ſome criminality—and muſt the guilt be aſcertained or puniſhed by the guilty? I am at a loſs, for the grounds of reaſon or authority, on which ſuch proceedings are founded.*

But I will ſuppoſe, the Houſe of Commons, choſen by ancient forms, however exceptionable, may be poſſeſſed of that power—is this the proper *ſeaſon*, for inviting its exertion? The corrupt influence which produced and ſupported the American War, is the immediate cauſe of the applications to Parliament on the ſubject of Repreſentation. And they are to be adjudged—by

---

* The Duke of *Richmond* attempted to bring in a Bill on this ſubject in the Houſe of Lords, as the foundation of a law—but he did not inform the Public whence Parliament derived the authority to enact ſuch a law.

whom?

whom? By the man, who was the inftrument of that corrupt influence. For the balancing power of the Houfe of Commons, is in the hands of Lord North.

It has been fuggefted by the enemies of Lord Shelburne,* that he means to haften this matter, to meet its fate; that it is his mode of rendering promifes to the People, confiftent with intereft at Court. But this is incredible. It is not even in Royalty to engender fuch villainy, on the moft corrupted ingredients of Faction. I muft afcribe it to precipitation, and want of judgment. The noble Lord may not like my choice in the alternative. Marks of imbecility have appeared in his adminiftration, which warrant the opinion—Lord North *calls* for the fubject, as a lion roars for his prey:—it is a reafon for with-holding it. Lord North's abilities and knowledge of the Conftitution, are not formidable: but he will carry the queftion, on a divifion of the Houfe.

Your Lordfhip may poffibly fay, what is to be done? I will anfwer—why fo impetuous— why in hafte? If a bridge were to be thrown over the river, it would be the fubject; not of

* The Letter was written in the Adminiftration of Lord *Shelburne*.

orations,

orations, but of sober or mature deliberation. Can you collect the sense of millions, and rear a fabric on their consent or judgment, by a few tumultuous evenings at taverns; where, I really think, it is impossible for reason or wisdom to be exercised? I will repeat here, what is so judiciously observed by Rousseau on another subject, " Lose as much time, as you can; " without letting the object escape you." The people are uninformed, or uninstructed in the business. They know only they are burthened and oppressed. Committees or Societies hold up *Resolutions* and political *Doctrines*, which embarrass, and rend them into parties. Let them be *instructed*: not by propositions requiring implicit assent; but by *directions to use their faculties*. It is the pretence, for with-holding the rights of the People; that their ignorance may abuse them. A method should be devised, to convey small, simple, and perspicuous publications into the hands of yeomen, farmers, and manufacturers. The nation, by such means, might be prepared to appoint a genuine and actual delegation, for the *immediate and sole purpose* of regulating Parliamentary Representation.

Such a delegation, would be truly, what those Conventions were *in effect*, which produced Magna Charta; and the Revolution. No man, under-

understanding the Constitution of England, will affirm, that Parliament, a mere legislative assembly, could have given *permanent authenticity* to such a deed as Magna Charta, or such an event as the Revolution. They were effected by the best *Conventions* that could be obtained of the whole kingdom; and nothing less than a national Convention can annul them. This is not the case with Acts of Parliament; much less with the resolutions of a particular House. They may be abrogated at pleasure, by succeeding Parliaments.—It is *here*, the measures in contemplation, of petitioning the Legislature, and bringing in Bills on the subject of equal Representation, appear *extremely unadviseable* or *dangerous*. If the bills or petitions be thrown out, the business may be lost. If carried through—precedents may be established, of unconstitutional and dangerous powers in Parliament—and the remedy prove worse than the disease. Let it be granted, that Parliament may regulate the mode of Representation—Liberty must be at an end. For though the Legislature may pass a popular Bill to establish its own power, it will soon repeal such a Bill, and on the same authority, vote itself independent of the people.

The *contrivance*, the *address*, the *wisdom*, requisite to form a Convention competent to the impor-

important bufinefs under confideration, are qualities uncommon, as they are more valuable, than the fuperficial, though brilliant talents, which form modern orators, or conftitute at this time, the pretenfions of Statefmen and Legiflators. It is one thing to lead a mob, of any rank or defcription : it is another to *produce* and to obey the will of the Public.

When fuch a Convention is formed—it will exprefs the opinion of the nation : and whether wife or erroneous; whether in favor of equal or of partial Reprefentation, it muft be *implicitly obeyed*. A nation may be miftaken in its interefts, as well as an individual : put it into a fituation to form and to exprefs its judgment; and its errors will lead it into wifdom.

I need not explain to a perfon of your Lordfhip's penetration that I mean by this Convention, a delegation from the counties and towns of Great-Britain, chofen by the majority of the inhabitants, by a fair ballot, and for the *only purpofe* of fettling the Reprefentation of the People— that the Delegation muft be effentally different in its nature and object from Parliamentary Reprefentation for the purpofes of civil regulations —that all conftitutional improvements; all deeds or charters of permanent obligation, which the

Legiflature

Legiflature cannot annul, have been made by affemblies of this kind, or *pretending to be* of this kind :—and that Parliaments; partial Affociations; and Committees of particular diftricts; if they could effect the beft purpofes in this bufinefs—being incompetent, and affording precedents, which would be immediately converted to the moft pernicious purpofes, might precipitately fink into Slavery the Nation *they meant to fave.*

I have the honor to be,

My LORD,

Your LORDSHIP's moft obedient Servant,

Feb. 25, 1783.

TO THE
ASSOCIATED CORRESPONDENTS
Of a Periodical Paper, called,
THE FRIEND OF THE PEOPLE.

GENTLEMEN,

YOU are requested to insert the following paper, at your first convenience.

> *Ma il volgo, nel cui arbitrio son gli onori,*
> *Che, come pare à lui, li leva, e dona;*
> *Ni dal nome del volgo voglio furio,*
> *Eccето l' uom prudente, trar persona;*
> *Che ne Papi, nè Re, nè Imperadori*
> *No ne trae Scettro, mitra, nè corona,*
> *Ma la prudenza, ma il guidicio buono;*
> *Grazie, che dal ciel date à pochi sono.*

But the base vulgar, who with judgment rude,
Gives honors and resumes, as fancy's shown;
Nor, from the name of vulgar, take I would,
Except the prudent person, any one;
For neither Pope, King, Emperor does exclude;
The mitre, or the sceptre, or the crown;
But prudence, solid judgment of the mind,
Favors which heaven but to the few has join'd.

TO THE PEOPLE.

IN the numerous addresses or dissertations relating to you, in antient and modern times, it has been difficult to understand, *Who you are?*

When

When the Athenian government was settled into a democracy—the people signified, citizens who amused themselves daily in hearing Orators deciding on public causes; and who had an allowance from the public treasure to keep them from starving. The Roman Empire, i. e. the whole known world at the time, was governed alternately by a venal Senate, and a mob, such as may be assembled on any day in Westminster Hall, or St. George's Fields, to chuse a senator, or to bait a bear.

In modern policy, the *People* has been every thing; any thing; or nothing; according to the views of political impostors. When a Turkish Emperor strangles a Vizir, for embezzling part of the public plunder; it is to relieve the people. When an English adventurer would jostle another, out of a lucrative place; it must be for the advantage of the people. All the good done, is by those who insultingly call themselves your servants: all the evil is fixed on you. The History of England, in almost every period, abounds with these perplexing absurdities. Charles the First, attempting to extinguish the rising sparks of liberty; sanctimoniously declared, it was for the love of his people. Oliver Cromwell put him to death, precisely on the same pretence: and the *Sin* has ever been left at the door of the people.

The House of Brunswick, in the first agitations of gratitude on its elevation to the English Throne, acquired such habits of rapidly repeating the phrase, that they seem like those of *Babbling*. Every thing since that event, has been *for the people*. The nation has been engaged in numerous Wars; *all* founded in injustice; but all for *your* benefit: your industry has been *accelerated* by accumulated *burthens*, to subsidize German Princes, or to create lucrative dependencies; and an army established to save you the trouble of guarding or securing your Liberties.

The American war was undertaken, not only for your *pecuniary* relief; but for your immediate *glory*: it was to give *you* subjects—a beautiful gradation of power or dominion being ordained; the soldiers (the first and most respectable order of citizens, according to the doctrine at court) being your masters; the Americans, the Irish, and the East Indians, your subjects, or slaves.

These good intentions, however, have been defeated; and a hundred millions of your money spent: but it will, no doubt, be consolatory, to know that the greater part has found its way into the pockets of those who were earnestly employed

ed in executing them. This, it must be confessed, has excited envy in the breasts of men, with whom necessity is the mother of genius, patriotism, and all the other virtues they possess. These circumstances have given rise to a war of opprobrious eloquence; terminated by the recent appointment of a ministry, with that wisdom which will ever distinguish his Majesty's reign: and, as private vices are public benefits, you may be assured, it will procure you the blessings which all possible combinations of ignorance, duplicity, profligacy, and avarice, can produce.

In these circumstances; and with such prospects, I wish precisely to understand; or rather to inform you, who I think you are. I profess myself your friend. I have nothing to hope or to fear from you. I desire only, in the few remaining years of a private life, to share with you, in the fragments of your splendid fortune.

In every community, where slavery is abolished—the first order of men, consists of those who occupy or cultivate the soil, and produce food. The second, of those who stimulate the former, whose invention and industry offer such conveniences as heighten the enjoyment of life. The third, of those who convey from one class, or from one nation to another, the produce of all kinds of talents. The fourth, of those employed to contrive and execute public regulations for the peace and prosperity of the state.— The first three classes, constitute *the People :* the fourth, is either a delegation, representing the other classes; or it is a factitious and spurious body, whose principle is diseased blood, and whose component parts, are all the vices which disgrace humanity.

Political evils arise from the operations of the fourth on all the other classes. If a delegation, it may betray its trust, and commit depredations by chicane or perfidy. If it should have pretensions of hereditary power, it must always be tyrannical or oppressive.

I need not therefore explain, what I mean by *the People :* or point out the classes, to which I profess myself a *Friend*.

As in the fermentations of natural bodies, a froth or scum will arise; so in the agitations or competitions of political classes, a worthless or vicious *Populace* may be produced. Persons mistaking the scum for the body which throws it off; or confounding the *Populace* with the *People,*

ple, are to be pitied or defpifed; not to be addreffed by reafon or perfuafion.

No period, in Hiftory, has been more interefting than the prefent. It feems teeming with grand events. New ftates are rifing, on new principles: while thofe who have given them birth, are languifhing in difeafes, or haftening to diffolution. No man, out of the froth of the community, can behold thefe things with indifference. He will either fly (with a fpirit participating of cowardice) to new and promifing regions: or fix his foot at the bafe of fome quivering pillar, and determine to fupport the fabric, or be buried in its ruins.

In either determination, it is hoped, the leffons to be given in this paper may be of important ufe.

Every misfortune, which is the object of public regret, may be traced into an encroachment of power, on the rights of the people. The firft impreffions of injury and violence admit only of partial or imperfect difcuffions. It may be ufeful at this time to revife, ftrengthen, and improve the feveral arguments advanced in favor of political and civil Liberty; and to lay them before the public in periodical papers.

The *Friend of the People* seems to be a paper on a public plan. On inquiry, I find the gentlemen, who have propofed themfelves as correfpondents, are unconnected with each other; and have one common object, the Political Liberty of the Conftitution, by a proper balance of its powers, and by a fair or equal reprefentation of the people. The perfons who felect, arrange, and revife the papers, are in circumftances, the leaft to be affected perhaps of any men in the kingdom, by the fluctuation of public events, and by the fate of perfons or parties.

None of thofe factions, therefore, which convulfe the public; no political denomination; no affociated body, however virtuous its principles; no club, fociety, or deputation, will be likely to controul, or direct the paper to partial or particular views. Correfpondents are invited, and folicited from every fociety and every quarter; but no political principles or meafures will be adopted and contended for, on any authority but that of reafon or argument. Every writer, may affume his fignature; and enjoy the gratitude or praife of the public at his own time, and in his own manner.

Whether

Whether a periodical paper, on such a plan, may attract your attention; or be of public service; a very little time will determine. The quivers of Satire and Lampoon, have been nearly exhausted, on public characters, with the same effect which clamour and hooting have on birds of prey, when their ravenous appetites are directed to their objects. Public offices or employments, are stakes to be contended for, differently in different periods: but not to be obtained in England, as the means of employing public talents or public virtues. As the times required variations in the arts of imposture, the masques of pretended patriots have been various: but they have generally worn masques. Now, they appear, in undisguised deformity. They feel, "there is no public,"—or, if there be, it is torpid, or insensible. Men who have violated *all possible* obligations; who have been guilty of frauds, robberies, blasphemies, and all kinds of crimes; men who have wasted the public treasure, and dismembered the commonwealth; come forward in open day, and with unblushing countenances, to solicit, to importune, to demand public confidence;—to be invested with powers which, if misemployed at this time, and they must be misemployed in such hands, may be fatal to the public interests.

Can *despair* in such circumstances, render the people of England listless or indifferent? Despair produces vigor, or violence. Any thing is better than sufferance and patience.

You will exclaim, " What can we do ? We " are oppressed or plundered by taxes and tax- " gatherers : and have such difficulties to subsist, " that if we divert our attention from our em- " ployments, our families must be undone."

When the English administration told the Americans, " you shall be slaves," the whole continent answered with one voice, " We'll die " an instant, not a lingering death." Thousands of them were starved or destroyed, to give life, liberty, and happiness to myriads.

" But, if *all* our rulers, are iniquitous and " abandoned, who can we substitute?"—Rulers! Who are your rulers? What, eight millions of Britons; renowned for liberty, knowledge, and virtue, at a loss for able or honest men, to do their public business, and leaving it a prey to characters most of which would dishonor Newgate! You have men, at this time, in the first offices of the state, who would have advantages by a comparison with Cartouch, or Jonathan Wild, Dr. Graham, or Katterfelto. But they can

can talk fix hours on a ftraw; or engage your attention for years, while they are folding up the diſhclouts of a kitchen. Thefe are all impoſtors or mountebanks. If they infeſted your pariſhes in the country, you would whip them from one to the other, by your common beadles. Yet you acquiefce in their feizing the helm of ſtate; at a time when the veſſel is nearly a wreck. Nay, you ſuffer the very man, who drove her on the ſhoals; who publickly plundered her while in his charge, to return into your fervice; without puniſhment, and without cenfure,

Look over to America—there fuch characters as now diſhonor your name throughout the earth, would foon be taught the meaning of the word *People.* Or turn to Ireland; where the inhabitants give you leſſons; which if you dare not follow,—*you deferve the confequences.*

A VOLUNTEER, in Correfpondence with

THE FRIENDS OF THE PEOPLE,

April 8, 1783.

TO THE

ASSOCIATED CORRESPONDENTS

OF THE

FRIEND OF THE PEOPLE.

Diligence and Carefulness are the Keys of Certainty. There is nothing so fearful unto wise men, but by Diligence and Care may be either happily prevented or remedied; nor is there any evil which may not fall on those who are indolent and careless.

GENTLEMEN,*

I ENTIRELY agree with the author of the letter to Lord Surrey, that, Parliament is not *constitutionally* competent to equalize the national representation. But, at the same time, I must observe, that it is equally incompetent to enact *any statute whatever*. So long as the House of Commons shall receive a majority of its members from less than seven thousand electors of petty boroughs, and so long as at least six parts in seven of the commons of the realm have no suf-

---

* This is not written by the Author of the Letters on Political Liberty; and it is inserted to introduce the Observations annexed to it by that Author.

frage at all, it would be trifling with words to call that house a representative of the people. If not their representative, it cannot of right make their laws. If, however, for peace sake, we submit to its other acts, why may we not acquiesce in a statute, for repealing all subsisting laws, and removing every obstruction, to *an equal representation* and *sessional elections?* Parliament, as now constituted, is at least as competent to undo mischief, as to do it. What should hinder its repealing the three most odious laws of our oppression; the statute of disfranchisement, the septennial and triennial acts? Those shackles removed, I would not object to its framing a statute for the future security of our liberties, because those liberties would not thenceforth depend upon *that* statute, but it would deprive future parliaments of *the means* of undermining them. Provided the people, particularly the unrepresented, will but continue their present exertions, I know that at least they will insure success; and whether their proceedings shall be correctly formal or not, I do not conceive that they will err so widely of their mark, as to let the substance of reformation escape them. As every one knows that Parliament will not reform itself, unless the people shew themselves determined to have it done, the act will of course be considered, as indeed it ought to be, not as an act of

the

the parliament, but as that of the people themselves; who, on such occasion, must be supposed to say, "You have as unconstitutionally pos-
"sessed yourselves of the forms of legislation, as
"you have wickedly exercised the functions.
"We will not, however, exert our supreme au-
"thority, in depriving you at once of the office
"you have assumed; because we are not will-
"ing to inflict on you that punishment for your
"usurpation, which, in such a case, we could not
"with propriety avoid. We therefore com-
"mand you before you retire, to add one more
"to the many acts you have passed,—*An act to
"put an end to your own power, and to restore the
"rights of the people.* This act, being the im-
"mediate effect of our known pleasure, would
"on that account have validity in the eyes of
"posterity; but we will remove all possibility of
"doubt, by confirming it by our instructions
"to the Parliament which we shall elect at your
"dissolution."—

If you shall think the following extract from a letter which I wrote to a *late* minister,* holds forth proper advice to the *present*, you are at liberty to print it, provided you esteem it worthy of the public eye.

+ Lord Shelburne.

"I CANNOT, my Lord, lay down my pen, without firſt expreſſing my hopes, that neither your Lordſhip nor Mr. Pitt, nor the other miniſters who may have adopted the great deſign of giving to your country a reformed legiſlature, have ſeen any ſufficient cauſe to accommodate your plan to the narrow ideas of party, or to the confined views of the ſelfiſh. Anxious as I am, not only on account of the reform itſelf, but of the reputations of thoſe under whoſe guidance it is to be brought about, I would adjure them duly to conſider the grand epoch in which they are to act. It is an epoch in which freedom for the firſt time has known the extent of its rights and diſcovered the means of their full eſtabliſhment. It is an epoch for a ſtateſman ambitious of great actions and true glory to ſit at the Britiſh helm. Great as was the national change in our ſiſter kingdom wrought under the conduct of Mr. Grattan, his fame is on the point of ſuffering an irreparable loſs, for having ſtopped in the career of his patriotiſm only a ſmall ſtep ſhort of his object.—Surely, my Lord, the ſame miniſters who are about to ſatisfy Ireland, even to the laſt ſcruple, will not by halves only eſtabliſh the rights of the Engliſh people! Surely they will be too wiſe to leave the nation in a ferment, until a complete eſtabliſhment muſt be made without either grace or glory in the act! Should any doubts

doubts of the practicability of a complete reform; should any apprehensions from the base part of Parliament; should any want of confidence in the people's affections, induce your Lordship and Mr. Pitt to propose any thing which should be evidently short of doing the people justice; your error I am persuaded would in the end prove less hurtful to the people than to yourselves. It was once, my Lord, your determination to unite with the Duke of Richmond whenever he should come forward again on the ground of parliamentary reformation, and to go as far as his Grace would go towards its completion.—Believe me, my Lord, I do not remind your Lordship of this declaration, from any idea that you now wish to go less far; but only from a fear that the confederated powers of pride, ignorance, and faction opposed to you, may have somewhat staggered your resolution. Interrupt and impede you they might; but their utter impotence to defeat your design, would only become the more apparent as they should the more dare to oppose you. The infamy of such an opposition would soon bring down upon them a nation's execrations and contempt, while it would raise your Lordship and the other leaders of the reform, high in the nation's esteem and veneration. And may I not observe, my Lord, that the minister who, in the present dilapidated state of our constitution,

stitution, should expect to restore its antient strength and grandeur without labour, without a contest, must rate the character of a national deliverer beneath its proper estimation? But, if I be not under the influence of some gross delusion, it will be found easier far to obtain, and deservedly to obtain that character, by effecting a complete reform, than to carry any partial measure that shall not be too insufficient to produce any good. If it be admitted that we actually depend upon the very rotten part of Parliament for the reforms we seek, it is absurd to seek any reform at all. But, if that rotten part is to yield to the voice of the nation, why, my Lord, in the name of conscience, is the reform to stop short of the nation's evident rights, of the nation's declared will upon full discussion; and the most mature deliberation? In respect to the nation at large, that discussion is as yet in its infancy. But its progress would be as the progress of a flame through the ripened corn, were but the public attention excited by an actual contest once commenced, whether the uncontrovertible rights of the nation should be established or not; while the people should see on their side (a novel sight indeed!) the king's principal ministers, supported by all the greatest characters in Parliament, as well as behold the metropolis and other great com-

communities amongſt themſelves already engaged in the cauſe; and, on the other ſide, ſhould diſcover only the deſpicable boroughs and their repreſentatives, who, although they might conſtitute a majority in the Houſe of Commons, would of courſe be conſidered as too inſignificant and contemptible to be permitted to make their will, and for their own diſhoneſt ends, a law of ſlavery to a great nation. Indeed, my Lord, it is a conteſt in which you could not fail to triumph. Your buſy enemies would then have nothing left but to hide their heads, and leave your Lordſhip in the undiſputed poſſeſſion of that popularity of which they have ſo induſtriouſly laboured to deprive you.

But, my Lord, putting your wiſhes as a patriot out of the queſtion, and conſidering you as a mere miniſter, I ſhould conceive that in the preſent ſtate of this country, and the relative condition of other nations, you muſt ſtand in need of the moſt complete legiſlative reform that can be imagined. Is not your monopoly of the commerce of America gone? Is not your controul over the trade of Ireland annihilated? Are you not ſinking under your own debt? Are not the diſcontents of Scotland breaking forth upon points which nothing ſhort of redreſs can in the

nature

nature of things ever give satisfaction, or prevent some serious mischief? And is not England daily growing more enlightened on the subject of its scandalous representation in Parliament, and fast approaching to that state in which *humble petitioners* will change their tone into that of *determined remonstrants?* Through the corruption of Parliament alone, does not corruption consequently pervade every department of government, and undermine all wholesome discipline? Then, with regard to the great rival powers of Europe, are not their improved commerce and increased navies objects of serious alarm to this debilitated country? Such a country, my Lord, under such circumstances, can neither be worth the future care of citizens, nor afford a prospect of satisfaction or glory to its minister, without a complete reform of its legislature.—She can neither hold a respectable existence amongst the nations, nor be to Majesty worth the ambition of reigning, unless her constitution be fully and unequivocally restored. Adhering but with spirit and firmness to the constitution, your Lordship may laugh at opposition, despise faction, and render the throne of your Sovereign once more the most glorious throne upon earth. A minister daring in right measures is the minister to please Englishmen! If at the same time he make the constitution his peculiar care, they will adore him. May your Lordſhip be that miniſter! With much reſpect, I have the honor to be,

My Lord,

Your Lordſhip's moſt obedient

humble ſervant,

I. C."

The Earl of Shelburne.

Remarks by the Author of the Letter to Lord Surrey.

THE preſent Writer ſeems to have the ſubject of parliamentary reform at heart, and to have conſidered it with attention. But he grants too much to the Author of the letter to Lord Surrey, if he means that Parliament ſhould interfere in the deciſion of its fate. That Writer graſps the whole buſineſs; and offers a complete and conſtitutional, but a daring, perhaps, hazardous plan. I. C. allows, Parliament is not competent to equalize repreſentation—yet urges

urges the expediency of leaving it to Parliament.

That the Legislature may repeal the statute of disfranchisement, the triennial and septennial acts, is true. It may also relinquish its usurpations on the people of England, as it has been obliged to do, on those of Ireland : and it should be *required*, to pass a solemn *Act of Renunciation*, of the kind insisted on by the Irish. Farther, it cannot proceed, (according to the general principle of Lord Surrey's correspondent, assented to by this writer) without resuming unconstitutional and dangerous powers.

The writer, I. C. seems to think, if applications for parliamentary reform succeed, it may not signify whether proceedings be strictly formal or not. If he means by formal, the etiquette of public assemblies, they are matters too insignificant to be brought into question : they are not hinted at, by the writer of the letter to the Earl of Surrey. He may mean, though cautious in expressing himself, success would justify the violation of constitutional principles. There is not an injunction of more authority and importance in scripture than " Do not evil that " good may come." Short-sighted moralists or politicians disobey this injunction ; and we find

find them always involved in regret, confusion, or misery. As in morals, no present benefit can be a compensation for the consequences of violating truth; so in politics, *no case can be stated justifying a violation of the evident, or essential principles of political œconomy.* When wise and honest men are tempted to admit expedients, they sink into the mob of *Political Sharpers.*

If Parliament be competent to decide on its own mode and terms of existence; the intended proceedings of the Duke of Richmond, Mr. Pitt, &c. should be countenanced. If it be not competent, which is the clear and avowed opinion of the writer of the letter to Lord Surrey: no time should be lost; no trouble should be spared, to prevent *their betraying the most important interests of the public* under the pretence of serving it.

It may be said, "the Duke of Richmond, Mr. "Pitt, &c. have so little prospect or desire of suc- "cess, that we have no reason to apprehend the "establishment of an unconstitutional precedent." The state of parties in Parliament, is not easily estimated. The objects of parliamentary leaders, without exception are power and emolument. To these, all principles; not of a public nature, because they are scouted; all principles which bind

fac-

factions, are sacrificed. If the factions, now in power, have made the sacrifice, because they would obtain power; who will affirm, the factions out of power, will not coalesce their political doctrines, or assimilate their discordant dialects, on some points, to drive off the present administration? What subject so proper for the purpose? what subject so popular, as the reform of Parliament? It slept in peace, during the administration of Lord Shelburne. But the Duke of Richmond and Mr. Pitt were not three days out of office, before they gave notice, they would bring the subject before Parliament; as the most likely to create disunion, in an administration formed by necessity, or to render it unpopular and odious; or to effect another revolution in the cabinet. Why, in such a case, may we not suppose, that Lord Gower will forget the prejudices of a Tory—Lord Thurlow his sonorous and empty jargon concerning the mysteries of a constitution he does not understand—and Lord Shelburne his sentimental politics: that all will coalesce with the Duke of Richmond, and declare for the people. The people will be the *stalking horse* of factions contending for power: and the stalking horse as usual will receive the injury.

We think therefore, in the present state of interested parties, there is some reason *to fear* the

the Duke of Richmond and Mr. Pitt, may be joined by the numerous enemies of the prefent adminiſtration; and may fucceed in giving a *mortal blow* to the conſtitution, by recognizing and eſtabliſhing a parliamentary right to model it, and to include or exclude the people at pleaſure.

If Parliament has betrayed its truſt, let it be adjudged, not by Parliament, but by a deputation of the people *for that purpoſe*. Nothing can be more abſurd, than delegates receiving powers for *ſpecial* purpoſes from the community; and accountable *to themſelves* for the uſe of thoſe powers.

TO THE

ASSOCIATED CORRESPONDENTS

OF THE

FRIEND OF THE PEOPLE.

TO THE KING.

Ουτε γαρ απιστειν πιστευουσιν, ουτε βασιλευειν,
Απιστουντων ηξιου. Plut. in Numb. p. 139.

I would not reign over a people whom I diftruft, or diftruft a people who have called me to reign over them.

MAY IT PLEASE YOUR MAJESTY,

IN the multitude of addreffes, prefented to your Majefty fince you afcended the throne, not many have been more unexpected; it is to be hoped, fome have been more unwelcome, than an application from a *real friend* of the *People of England*. It is probable, you have ever been unacquainted with perfons of that character; or that you have found pretenders to it, the moft unprincipled and abandoned of men.

A line has been drawn around your Majefty, within which, *not one of the People of England* may have

have set his foot: and at this day, after a reign of twenty years, you may be as much a stranger to them, as to the people of China.

Those classes, on whose talents, industry, or labor, the community subsists, are not to be known by a residence in royal palaces, by short excursions in the company of sycophants around Windsor, or by driving like a courier to a naval review at Portsmouth; yet this is the description of your Majesty's travels: and it was hardly possible to contrive them, more effectually to preclude opportunities of information or knowledge.

The crouds that hang on the wheels of your carriages; that choak up the roads or streets as you pass; and risque their wretched lives to look at you—merely to ascertain your form to be human—your courtiers tell you, are the People: it is your Majesty's misfortune to believe them. If the artifice had not been practised on you in early infancy, it would not have had the effect, which all considerate Englishmen deplore: for all the evils of England, are owing to your Majesty's not knowing *your People*. Early associations are not to be broken, even in strong minds. Darkness recalls fears in men, who have discarded the opinions which first occasioned them; and the word *people* brings to your Majesty's jesty's imagination, the city mob attempting the life of Lord Bute; the ragged and abandoned populace stopping the Queen to view her person; and the robbers, or pick-pockets, who stormed in the streets and insulted your guards for Wilkes and Liberty.

If your Majesty had ever contemplated, at leisure, the farmer's family in its various occupations; or the artist regulating the industry of his mechanics; and had received the true impression of their characters or manners—you would have avoided this error, so fatal to the reputation of your country:—you would have seen the difference, between the great and numerous classes of the industrious, *who are the People*, whose employments keep them in their stations—and the dissipated, idle, or wretched crowds, which infest large towns, and resort to all spectacles:—you would have seen, that a courtier is not at a greater distance from truth; a gambler (though of your Majesty's cabinet) from honesty and *real wisdom*; a patriot by trade, from public spirit; or a pedagogue transformed into an archbishop, from Christian meekness—than the mobs and tumultuous assemblies, which have disgusted your Majesty, from the great, respectable, and, to you, invaluable body, of *the People of England*.

I should

I should exceed the limits of this paper, if I were to point out, to your Majesty, all the obvious and melancholy consequences of such misapprehensions.

The word *People*, calls up unpleasing emotions in your Majesty's countenance; it impresses instant apprehension or terror on the the Queen; and the royal children imbibe prejudices, which may be their inconvenience or misfortune. This error prevents all communication between your Majesty and the community, but through vile or corrupt channels; and is the reason, though of exemplary virtue in private character, you have ever been surrounded by a succession of the most despicable miscreants, which have dishonored the councils and public offices of any country.

It was the limited sphere of your Majesty's political knowlege; it was the false information brought to you in that sphere; and particularly the credit you gave to misrepresentations of *your* People,—that induced you to let loose the dogs of war, among the numerous herds and folds of your own family, and separated America from your dominion for ever.

A similar error induced your Majesty to rest the security of your person and family; the ultimate appeal of all the branches of the executive power;—not to the force of the community at large; but to a mercenary army, composed of the refuse or dregs of the land.

A similar error, may render your Majesty indisposed, if it be true you are indisposed, to an equal representation of the people. No man in England has an interest, which can be put in comparison with that of your Majesty, in the accomplishment of that important or necessary event:—it is from a wish that you may fully perceive or understand this interest, I am tempted to address your Majesty.

The meanest clerk in any of your offices, has not submitted to so much drudgery or labor; hardly a convict in your prisons can have felt equal anxiety or misery, with your Majesty; during the follies, iniquities, errors, and misfortunes of your ministers, in a reign of two and twenty years. These ministers have ever been the offspring of factions; controling the throne by menace or intrigue, while they employed its influence or revenue to degrade the English legis-

legislature, and blot out the honorable epithets annexed to the English name.

Factions are swarms of locusts, hovering between you and the People; obscuring or confounding your views: and though at enmity with each other, pursuing a common object, in dishonoring your character or government, and plundering or oppressing your kingdom. Though the pecuniary grants to your Majesty have surpassed all examples in history, every branch of your revenue is loaded with debts; your domestic arrangements are on a scale unbecoming your situation; and the small expence of them, shamefully discharged. You are lodged, as in one of the out-houses of your ancestors; and, instead of having a table suited to your dignity, you board with the Queen at a moderate and stated price.

Can there be any gratification, in your intercourse with despicable or interested factions, to balance these sacrifices and mortifications? Each of them amuses you with hopes of being something more than King of England; and on being forced out by a competitor, always leaves you something * * * *.

It

It seems you have not sufficient employment for your servants, in your executive capacity; they always imprefs on your mind the neceffity of having at your will, or in your particular way of thinking, a majority of the legiflature: without this, they fay, no public bufinefs can be done; i. e. your Majefty's minifters cannot make the laws as well as execute them.

What fcenes of perplexity and mifery muft your Majefty be involved in? You rife early; you fit up late; you eat the bread of carefulnefs and forrow—to what purpofe? Do you hear the murmurs of poverty, labour or induftry, from every quarter of your kingdom? Do they fcatter any thing like the dews of heaven over your anxious and agitated mind? You hear the difcordant clamors of contending or interefted factions; and by harboring their feveral leaders in fucceffion, your name or authority is ufed to diflionorable purpofes, by the greateft enemies of your crown and family: for there are not in Europe, men capable or difpofed to do your Majefty the injuries, done by thofe heads of parties which infult your throne, or find their account in iniquitous meafures committed in your name.

Difcard

Discard all these pests of the community. Bolt the gates of your palaces against them! Suspend the functions of government, rather than suffer them to be at the will, or for the purposes of parties. Call on your people for the first time in your life:—you will find them a rock of adamant, on which you may collect the broken parts of your constitutional power in security and peace. Invite a fair or just representation of your country: and after making a present of Lord North to the Americans; of Lord Shelburne to the Irish; of Lord Mansfield to St. Peter; and Lord Bute to ———; fixing Thurlow as master of Westminster School; and giving Fox and Pitt the Pantheon, as a theatre of public debate—you might meet your Parliament unmolested; and with a pleasure you have never experienced

It may occur to your Majesty; or it may be suggested by your cabinet, if you withdraw the influence which gives the disposal of public resolutions, or the formation of laws, into the hands of your servants; and summon such a representation of the People as may constitute an independent assembly, capable of deliberation or of preparing laws for your assent;—this assembly may impede your operations and curtail your

your power. It is the bufinefs and intereft of fuch men as ufually furround your Majefty, to confound ideas effentially diftinct. What underftanding can infer, that Parliament by being rendered independent muft become inimical to your Majefty? The tranfition is eafy from dependence to enmity; not from independence.—Your power or prerogatives, inftead of being diminifhed, would be multiplied. In the relation you ftand to thofe political clufters, which contend for the advantage of acting in your name; you do not enjoy the liberty of a citizen; much lefs the power of an Englifh king. You cannot appoint a page or a footman, without the confent of the faction of the day. This is attributed to the nature of the Englifh conftitution, with which it has not the flighteft relation. No prince in Europe, would have fo much liberty or fo much power as an Englifh king, underftanding the bounds prefcribed to him by the conftitution. Boundlefs power, befides being ridiculous in every attempt to poffefs it, is always participated in a manner fo indefinite, as to create perpetual jealoufy and unhappinefs. The provinces of human talents fhould be afcertained; and the more accurately it be done, the offices of life muft be the more practicable and the more conducive to happinefs. This is the peculiar privilege of an Englifh king; and he could not have enemies

of

of his glory or peace, more malignant or injurious, than thofe who would lead him out of his province, to impede or render ineffectual the other parts of the conftitution. By aiming to make him, the legiflator, the judge, as well as the executive magiftrate, they clog all the wheels of the machine ; and it is with great induftry, even in mifchief, they deduce private emoluments from fuch meafures.

Let your Majefty delineate in imagination, the different effects, not only to your country but to yourfelf, from reftoring the balance or harmony of the Conftitution—and you will foon form your determination. To deftroy the privileges of the Commons, almoft all the prerogatives of the crown are facrificed—*To What ? To Whom ?* To groups of a nobility; the ridicule or fcorn of Europe. In other kingdoms, the nobles have antient defcent, hereditary honors, and claims founded on fplendid fervices. In England, a profeffion, the effence of which is fineffe or knavery, furnifhes moft of thofe rank and numerous weeds which now fhade the few honorable plants to be feen around you. Is it not fufficient they have fpoiled or plundered your people in the way ? Is it neceffary you fhould facrifice yourfelf and your moft
valuable

valuable interests, to adorn mushrooms, the produce of filth and villainy?

I speak not against the honors of nobility, as the rewards of virtue; and I can suppose a House of Lords might be an useful part of the Constitution. But when it acts; sometimes in possession of the prerogatives of the King, sometimes leading the House of Commons in its train,—it must be deemed an atrocious evil.

It is to this evil, your Majesty should immediately attend. Set the House of Commons free from the dominion of the Lords, by inviting and encouraging *your People* to send up a representation of the kingdom. The heads of factions may have the audacity to menace, until the deputies arrive: which will be the first moment of your real liberty or power; and will consign those parties that torment you, and rob the public, to eternal dishonor.

If your Majesty regard the glory of your name; the peace of your mind; the prosperity of your family; the security and happiness of the people committed to your government—lose no time, in doing every thing in your power, to obtain a conſtitutional legiſlature, by an actual and complete deputation from all the inhabitants of your kingdom.

I am, with more truth, than may be told your Majeſty in many years—your Majeſty's very dutiful and obedient ſubject:

But a real and determined
FRIEND of the PEOPLE.

The preceding letters and papers, effected a ſchiſm in the creed of the political reformers; who had been unanimous in their reſolutions to petition Parliament, to renounce its uſurpations or to reform itſelf. Some of them, in their correſpondence with the Iriſh Volunteers, expreſſed doubts of a ſimilar tendency with the ſentiments the author had ſtated. Theſe doubts ſerved only to increaſe the perplexities of an heterogeneous body; which had neither information or virtue to effect its oſtenſible purpoſe. A character in it, drew the attention of Europe, by ſtrong and daring profeſſions of public principles. The following letter and reſolutions were conveyed to that political Bobadil; and they had probably ſome effect in terminating his bravadoes.

IF

Dec. 31, 1783.

IF the measures lately taken by the delegates of the Irish Volunteers had succeeded in producing a parliamenty reform; though I should have disapproved them in my own mind, I should not have taken the liberty of giving you any trouble on the subject. But as they have failed, for the same reason similar attempts have failed in England, that of admitting Parliament to be party and judge in a question between Parliament and the Community: and I see by some resolutions in Ireland, as well as by letters from English correspondents, that sentiments, principles, phrases and expressions are adopted, which, on the first publication of the Pamphlet I have the honor of sending you, were deemed visionary, impracticable, or presumptuous:—I hope I shall be excused if unsolicited or unsought, I offer some little assistance in prosecuting a plan, which I had first the honor of suggesting in this country, and which alone, in my opinion, can produce parliamentary representation without giving up the most essential principle of a free constitution.

I passed through a great part of Ireland last summer, and took every opportunity to urge the reasons I had often in England offered in vain, against petitions or applications of any kind to Parliament to reform itself. But I found only a few who could perceive the uncontroled power of Parliament in civil regulations, while the circumstance of its being a delegation for civil purposes, must render it totally incompetent to determine on fundamental or constitutional arrangements.—They who did perceive the limits of Parliamentary power, were not prepared for a measure in their opinion so bold, as that of disputing its encroachments: and to be furnished with courage, they waited for the affront I foretold Parliament would offer, to the very humiliating condescension of its constituents or masters. One gentleman seemed disposed to assume the character or to speak the language of a constituent; and when I had drawn up the following Resolutions, undertook to move them at the meeting of the delegates of Leinster. I left Dublin a few days before the meeting took place; and not observing any intimation of such a measure in the printed accounts of its proceedings, I presumed his heart failed him; or he was advised to drop the pretensions of a free citizen, and to acquiesce in the general resolution of petitioning those, whose claims to be even the deputies or stewards of the community were questionable. To petition the

the legislature, is the privilege and happiness of a free citizen; or of any collective description of citizens, making parts of the community: but when the whole community speaks, its words are fundamental laws, annihilating all inferior authorities. It is to avoid the inconveniences attending the movements or actions of the whole body, that powers are delegated to legislatures, senates, or kings. But no state is free which cannot, in its collective capacity, resume or regulate those powers at pleasure. A whole community, having pretensions to liberty, petitioning its deputies, is an appearance so ridiculous, so absurd, and bordering so nearly on impossibility, that it would be incredible in any thing but the political conduct of mankind. If these papers can be of any use in the measures you are pursuing, for the advantage of your country, I shall be fully rewarded. Though I have some gratification in seeing many of those persons who deemed the advice to the community to regulate the power of its stewards as speculative or factious, gradually adopting the opinion or uttering it as their own: yet having no private interest or passion to serve in the business, my pleasure will arise from the use or advantage which any of these hints may be of; not from any notice which can be taken of them. The manner in which the letters of correspondents to the delegates of the Irish volunteers have been held up to public attention here and in Ireland, has incurred the imputation of vanity, and been of disservice to the interest they were intended to favor.

An object of such magnitude as the just representation of the community, is not to be greatly benefitted by the publications of hasty suggestions or declamatory exhortations. The opinions or observations of sensible men might have been of service to those who were appointed in Ireland to deliberate on the measures to be taken; but in the important period of that deliberation, to circulate them in the newspapers of England and Ireland, in hand-bills or pamphlets, had a tendency to misemploy the attention of the people; or to force them into parties and speculations on subjects they were not to discuss, because they had consigned them to their delegates.

I have my doubts that the friends of political Liberty will yet succeed in their liberal and beneficent views; and I think there is more to be apprehended from their haste to obtain *some* object by *any* means, than from their total discomfiture or disappointment. Expedients or compositions apparently prudent, are the bane of all

all political proceedings. We should not attempt any thing, not to be obtained on just or reasonable principles. If the community cannot control its stewards, or point out in the style of a master the conditions of their services, it is not free; and its services cannot be much alleviated by any thing it may obtain by humiliation or servility.

In this undertaking, we should have in our eye, the advice of the great Lord Bacon, " to carry ourselves soberly and usefully in moderate things; to sow the pure seeds of pure truth for posterity; and not be wanting in our assistance to the first beginning of great things."

I have the honor to be, &c.

RESOLUTIONS.

I.

THAT a reprefentation of the people in Parliament being a delegation or truft, the power muft be in thofe who delegate; not in thofe who are delegated, to fpecify the conditions, or to limit the duration of truft: the reprefentatives being at liberty, as in all conventions of a fimilar kind, to accept the conditions, or to decline the truft.

I fhall move this refolution, not only becaufe I know it to be confiftent with reafon, and the uniform experience of mankind in all agreements or contracts; but becaufe I fee with concern and mortification, thofe perfons who have been confpicuous in the firft fteps towards the emancipation of Ireland, and even corps of volunteers, difpofed to follow the example of England, in chufing delegates or fervants, and then *humbly* or *abjectly* petitioning thofe fervants to allow them reafonable conditions or terms. This is not meant as a reflection on the people of England, who, as individuals, I esteem among the best informed and respectable people on earth; but on those aristocratic leaders or pretended patriots, who have long been in possession of the springs of their constitution, and who, under the forms or denominations of Liberty, have supported a ruinous species of government, which has divided the commonwealth, and ignominiously sunk its name and credit. These leaders of parties, in England, have anxiously watched every disposition in the people, to throw off the tyranny of a Parliament; which, while it called itself omnipotent, or trampled on the rights of Englishmen (their constituents and masters) in England, Ireland, and America, consisted of the creatures and tools of an aristocracy in collusion with the minister of the crown. When associations were made, or societies formed for the restoration of popular rights; many of these aristocratic chiefs, adopted their views with apparent zeal and avidity. They insinuated themselves into all those societies, and by dazzling their imaginations or warping their judgement, (the present effect of oratory) took the lead in their measures. Hence, I should suppose, the general prevalence in England of that absurdity, which leaves with Parliament, and consequently with the proprietors, of Parliament, the power of favoring

or

or destroying the Liberties of its country with impunity. I suppose it to be owing to such influence: because, while associations or societies have been uttering resolutions of this pernicious tendency; and orators, in Parliament have acquired fame by declaiming on them; they have been reprobated, as absurd or unconstitutional in perspicuous and masterly publications.

It is to be apprehended, that causes of a similar nature will have similar effects in Ireland. The general election has taken place, almost every where, under the influence or direction of the Irish aristocracy: the House of Commons will therefore be the instrument of that aristocracy, which may be conveniently susceptible of intrigue or management from an artful administration. The influence of the aristocracy seems to have perverted the public views, after the example of England; for all resolutions, propositions, or petitions are to be referred to Parliament, the creature or tool of the aristocracy: the pretended delegates and attornies of the people, are apparently to act as their absolute masters or proprietors; and the legislature is to be party and judge. Under the present impression of public opinion, it may vote short Parliaments; but having established a precedent, it will probably on some future and fatal

fatal occasions, vote whatever may be pleasing or convenient to its masters.—It is not agreeable therefore to the evident or indisputable principles of reasoning on political subjects; it is not agreeable to the original and genuine views of the English constitution, which have been adopted in Ireland: it is not safe, prudent, or consistent with the plans of political and civil Liberty held out by the friends of their country to the people of Ireland, to take from them the power of proposing or ascertaining the terms and conditions on which they will be represented in Parliament.

II.

Resolved therefore, that the people of Ireland ought; and that this country shall, furnish a precedent, by unanimously agreeing to require, that the sessions of Parliament be annual, and that the Parliament itself continue no longer than   years.

I shall move this resolution; because it is not improperly controling Parliament, as is plausibly pretended by those who wish to exclude the people of Ireland, from their proper influence in the constitution. The general conditions of Parliamentary delegation, should be clearly specified

cified or afcertained: but when Parliament is once chofen and affembled, its refolutions fhould be its own; uncontrouled or uninfluenced by the people. Conftituents forming Parliaments, without conditions of truft; and then wifhing to direct their particular refolutions, feem to have no clear ideas of the political power of a free people, or of the office and duty of reprefentatives. The requifitions of the people fhould be confined to the terms of appointment, truft, or duration; not to fpecific votes or laws in Parliament; which being confined to civil or municipal duties, would never fport with or endanger the conftitution and people of Ireland.

III.

Refolved, That in the prefent ftate of this country, the Irifh volunteers muft ftand for *The People*; and that their requifitions muft be regarded as thofe of the people of Ireland.

The condition of the Roman Catholics is not thought to admit of total emancipation. Every freeholder in Ireland is, or ought to be, a volunteer: the exceptions to this general rule are fo few, and of fuch a nature, that it will hardly offend againft the moft accurate truth, to say, the volunteers consist of all the freeholders; i. e. all the free people of Ireland. They are armed, it is true: but all citizens who would be free, should be armed; and the collective body of a nation, should not only be in a condition to defend itself against foreign enemies; but to hold within the limits of their obligations or their duties, the several orders of its government; which—uncontrouled, unawed, and without the apprehension of responsibility, always become its most mischievous enemies. The requisitions of the volunteers, in the present situation of things, and the conditions of trust or delegation they may prescribe to Parliament, must be regarded as the will of the people of Ireland.

IV.

Resolved, That those persons, chosen to sit in Parliament, who shall not acquiesce in the will of the people of Ireland, expressed by the unanimous, or general resolutions of all its corps of volunteers, shall be deemed disqualified by the refusal of the conditions prescribed for Parliamentary trust; and their seats be directed to be filled, by persons who will, *bona fide*, be the representatives or agents of the people; not the brokers of an aristocracy in its dealings with an English cabinet, or its deputed instruments and tools.

ON the discomfiture of the Irish proceedings, the hopes of parliamentary reform were generally relinquished. The petitioners of Parliament lost their credit; political partizans finding them of little utility, and the business terminated in a specious effort, by the minister, Mr. Pitt, probably intended to impose on public credulity; to induce the delegated power, to give laws to the supreme; to mangle its parts, and lop off its members with puerile or fantastic wantonness.

If the present disposition to peace should continue; if a spirit of cultivation and industry raise the people into circumstances of ease or the capacity of consideration; impostors will cease to delude, who gratify their vanity, ambition, or avarice, by misleading embarrassed ignorance, or exciting false hopes in unsuspicious credulity.

The manœuvres of political adventurers of every rank and description have been directed to involve in difficulties, or to reserve in their hands, the subject of parliamentary representation;

tion; being fully aware that the actual deputies of a powerful and opulent nation, would not be guided by the views of gamblers, or the declamations of venal orators. The interests created by intrigue or corruption in Parliament, are numerous and powerful: they are most powerful where least suspected; among those members called *independent* country gentlemen. The tool of a borough is understood; or the opulent mushroom, who buys a seat, means to make himself a gentleman, and is not always disposed to sell: but the country gentleman, has numerous relations and friends, an extensive interest to support, he therefore has his eye on the incidents of the law, the church, the army, the customs and excise: no member of Parliament is so susceptible of corrupt influence as the country gentleman.

The most determined resistance to reform, must be expected from a legislature whose venal habits and interests would be interrupted or destroyed by it: and our hopes must be directed to the gradual information and improvement of the people.

THE END.

www.ingramcontent.com/pod-product-compliance
Lightning Source LLC
Chambersburg PA
CBHW031335160426
43196CB00007B/702